Ivies

Ivies

Peter Q. Rose, NDH

BLANDFORD PRESS
Poole   Dorset

First published in the UK 1980

Copyright © 1980 Blandford Press Ltd,
Link House, West Street,
Poole, Dorset, BH15 1LL

British Cataloguing in Publication Data
Rose, Peter Q
  Ivies.
  1. Ivy
  I. Title
  635·9′33′687   SB413.184

ISBN 0 7137 0969 3

Printed in Great Britain by Butler & Tanner Ltd, Frome, Somerset
Colour by Tonbridge Printers, Tonbridge, Kent.

Contents

Foreword

The common ivy, *Hedera helix*, is so much part of our environment growing in woodland, on buildings or in hedgerows that we do not always appreciate the merits of its numerous variants in the garden. As with so many garden plants the ivy has been subject to the fickle phases of horticultural fashion but during the last thirty years has steadily regained the popular esteem in which it was held during the Victorian era.

In spite of the undoubted popularity of ivies as house plants and for various uses in the garden no major work on the genus has been produced in Britain since that by Shirley Hibberd more than a century ago. The plethora of cultivar names given to ivies since Hibberd's time has led to very considerable confusion as inevitably new ivies pass from grower to grower and in the process obtain different and usually invalid names. Various attempts to clarify the complicated nomenclatural tangles have been made but with only moderate success to date. Happily, Peter Rose has now provided gardeners and nurserymen with an authoritative and accurate work which sets out clearly many of the problems and solves others.

It is apparent that the author has spent a great deal of time in tracing the history and origins of the ivy cultivars described and this book contains much information that is not available elsewhere or is only to be found by diligent searching of the literature. In particular the provision of comparative descriptions, frequently of cultivars only poorly documented previously, will be invaluable in setting a pattern by which the descriptions of new introductions may be judged.

Ivies is by no means confined to historical and descriptive accounts and contains in addition much useful information on all aspects of ivy cultivation. The author has produced an excellently blended mixture of practical and theoretical knowledge which should both instruct and stimulate the ordinary gardener whilst providing the ivy enthusiast with a standard reference point for the future.

Chris Brickell
Director, Royal Horticultural Society's Garden, Wisley
Chairman, International Nomenclature Code for Cultivated Plants

Preface

Despite the fact that ivy is now known over a great part of the world, it is thought of traditionally as a typically British plant, and yet this is the first comprehensive book devoted to the plant to be published in Britain since that of Shirley Hibberd in 1872.

In that long time-span new varieties have arisen and new uses have been found for the plant in garden, home and landscape: a book on the subject is certainly overdue. As a Plant Health Inspector for the Ministry of Agriculture my attention was drawn not only to the merits of the plant, which do warrant a book in themselves, but also to its confused nomenclature. This book is the result of some twelve years' spare-time study of the subject as well as the exchange of varieties and information with ivy enthusiasts from many countries.

One hundred and twenty-five varieties are described here in detail, many for the first time in a published work, and over sixty of the most useful are depicted in colour. This is by no means the total of varieties; there are probably at least two hundred in existence at the present time. Ivy specialists will note various omissions; some of these are varieties of whose correct name I am at present in doubt, others are those whose horticultural value makes them unworthy of inclusion. The names of the varieties have in the past been extremely muddled, to the confusion of nurserymen, landscape architects and gardeners everywhere. This book seeks to clarify this situation and describe the virtues of a plant that is beginning to enjoy a world-wide popularity akin to that which it enjoyed in Victorian Britain.

Acknowledgements

'No man is an island' and anybody who sets out to examine or comment on any genus of plants will owe much to those who have gone before as well as to those of his contemporaries who so readily make available material and information.

I freely acknowledge my debt to the former. Of the very many in the latter category I am particularly indebted to the following:

Chris Brickell, Director, Royal Horticultural Society's Gardens, Wisley;

Ingobert Heieck, Brother in Charge of Neuburg Monastery Nursery, Heidelberg, Germany;

Dr Peter A. Hypio, L H Bailey Hortorium, Ithaca, USA;

Roy Lancaster, Curator, Hillier Arboretum, Winchester;

Harry van de Laar, Horticultural Officer, Research Station for Arboriculture, Boskoop, Holland;

Alison Rutherford;

Don and Beth Savage;

Henri Schaepman, President, American Ivy Society, Elkwood, USA;

Robert Scase, Sometime Librarian, Royal Horticultural Society's Gardens, Wisley;

Peter Stageman, Librarian, Lindley Library, London,

and Mrs Sylvia Timms.

Their help, information and advice has been invaluable; any errors in the translation of it into book form are my own.

Last but never least to my wife who, with Ivy a permanent resident in the home, has survived this *ménage à trois* so well and helped me in so many ways with advice and constructive criticism.

Photographs 1–54 are by Don Savage; 55 by Michael Clift, and 56–71 by Robin Fletcher.

Introduction

Few plants can be so familiar to so many people as the ivy. The shape of its leaf, its clinging habit and its liking for shade have been commented upon by writers and poets through the ages. Its early introduction from Europe into North America extended the range of people who, though they may know no other plant, are able to recognise ivy. From earliest times ivy has been a familiar plant in Europe; indeed if the European Economic Community were seeking a floral emblem it could do worse than choose ivy, common to all member states, encircling and supporting itself and others.

In mythology ivy was associated with Bacchus and Bacchanalian orgies. Along with some other things associated with pagan practices it was incorporated into Christian ritual: in this case into the Christmas garlands made to celebrate the anniversary of Christ's birth. The holly and the ivy became traditional Christmas decorations as some of the old carols remind us. From the time of Chaucer until well into the Middle Ages a 'bush' of ivy hung on a pole indicated a tavern. The custom came from the Romans and spread throughout Europe. The sign was called an 'Alepole' or 'Alestake'. Chaucer, describing the Sompnour (Summoner) in *The Canterbury Tales*, says, 'A garland hadde he sette upon his hede, as gret as it were for an Alestake.' With this in mind it is pleasant to note that the foremost ivy nursery in America at the present time calls itself 'The Alestake'. Incidentally, it is from the custom of hanging the 'bush' of ivy on a pole that the phrase 'good wine needs no bush' arises, meaning that a good product needs no advertisement: the phrase is common in several languages.

The ivy's tenacity has inspired poets through the ages but few more eloquent than Charles Dickens who in his charming poem *The Ivy Green* wrote:

> The brave old plant in its lonely days
> Shall fatten upon the past,

For the stateliest building man can raise,
Is the ivy's food at last.
Creeping on where time has been,
A rare old plant is the ivy green.

Certainly ivy can attain great age. Records of a plant growing at Ginac near Montpellier in France show it to be four hundred years old. The poet's line 'Is the ivy's food at last', however, is not so accurate: it brings to mind the controversy that has spasmodically enlivened gardening papers, newspapers and horticultural journals for the last 140 years and now occasionally crops up on television. This is the question as to whether or not ivy harms or benefits trees and walls. Ivy is not a parasitic plant: the small rootlets put out by the climbing shoots help the plant to adhere to its support; if moisture is available in the bark crevices or the bricks and mortar it is likely that they can absorb it, but they have no penetrative powers. With regard to trees, ivy clings to its host; it does not feed on it, and while the tree is in good health the ivy will be a secondary plant and although ascending the trunk and branches can do no harm. Should the tree decline for any reason and fail to leaf, the ivy will take over as is often seen on elms killed by Dutch Elm Disease.

On sound house walls ivy is harmless, indeed beneficial, keeping them dry in winter and cool in summer – an economical form of insulation. It can, however, harbour flies and insects and to offset this should be clipped over in late spring. This clipping improves the ivy and maintains a neat and effective wall covering. Walls that are very weak can be pulled down if a weight of ivy has bushed out at the top of the wall and then becomes heavy with snow or rain and susceptible to the pull of strong winds. Clipping obviates this possibility and indeed the life of many walls could be prolonged by a well-managed ivy cover.

Ivy has a long history as a garden plant. Pliny the Elder in his *Natural History* tells us that Theophrastus, around 314 BC, stated that it did not grow in Asia Minor, but that Alexander had come back from India with his army wearing wreaths of ivy because of its rarity. Pliny describes the plant in some detail: 'It is the helix which has most varieties of all as it differs greatly in leaf; three are most noticeable, the grass green helix which is the commonest, a second kind with a white leaf and a third with a variegated leaf.' This must be the first recorded description of a variegated ivy. He mentions also a stiff ivy which will stand without a prop. This refers I think to the 'Tree Ivy' rather than the erect types of ivy that we grow on rock gardens.

Although the common ivy is frequently mentioned in literature there seems to be no record of variations of the common ivy being planted. Despite this it is unlikely that inquisitive mankind would overlook an ivy with, say, particularly interesting fingered leaves or variegation and yet, following Pliny, no more is heard of ivy varieties until the eighteenth century when in 1770 Richard Weston in his *Universal Botanist and Nurseryman* listed the following:

Hedera – Ivy (Fr. Lierre)
1 *Helix*
2 *Argenteo variegata* – the silver striped ivy
3 *Aureo variegata* – the gold striped ivy
4 *Poetica baccis luteis* – yellow berried archipelagian ivy
5 *Canadensis scandens* – Virginia creeper

The last was classified as an ivy in error by botanists at that time: in fact it belongs to a different plant family.

The first catalogue reference to ivies appears to be that of John and George Telford of York who in 1775 listed 'Ivy – Striped' at 6*d* per plant; it is interesting to note that they listed the Early Red Honeysuckle at 2*d* per plant. I suspect the 'Striped Ivy' to be the variety we know as 'Cavendishii'. Telford's listing was followed by that of William and John Perfect of Pontefract, Yorkshire in 1777, also listing 'Ivy Striped'. Peter Lauder of Bristol in 1795 listed 'Ivy – Variegated' and in 1815 George Lindley of Norwich listed three: *helix, foliis variegatis* and *hibernica*, this last being the first catalogue reference I have found to the Irish Ivy. Loddiges, the celebrated nurseryman of Hackney, London, listed four in 1820, and in 1826 seven, *viz. Hedera helix* 'arborescens' (the Tree Ivy), 'digitata', 'fol. argentea', 'fol. aurea', 'fructu-alba', 'maculata', 'poetica'. 'Fructu-alba' would presumably be the white-berried ivy mentioned by various writers but always at second-hand; no one seems to have actually seen it.

Interest in ivies slowly increased and by 1846 Peter Lawson & Son of Edinburgh were listing twelve varieties. In 1859 W. G. Hen-

13

derson of St John's Wood, London, listed sixteen, and by 1865 that number had increased to thirty-nine. In Germany the nursery firm of Haage & Schmidt who were building up an international plant trade issued a catalogue in 1868 listing twenty-three varieties, and in 1867 William Paul, the distinguished and conscientious London nurseryman, listed his collection 'of more than forty sorts' with descriptions, in the 'Gardener's Chronicle' of 30 September. His names were authenticated and published in Germany by the botanist Karl Koch and provided a basis for the names of cultivated ivies. A new species *Hedera colchica* had reached Britain in the 1840s from the Odessa Botanic Garden. Introduced as *Hedera roegneriana* the name commemorated M. Roegner, the Director of the Botanic Garden at that time, but the name was never properly published and in 1859 Koch, realising that it was the same plant as that found much earlier by the botanist Kaempfer and later by Wallich and by Koch himself, described it as *Hedera colchica*. The Canary Island Ivy *Hedera canariensis* and the Himalayan Ivy *Hedera nepalensis* were introduced about the same time; the former was confused with the Irish Ivy *Hedera helix* 'Hibernica' and this confusion, coupled with rather brief descriptions, makes the identification of some of the early ivy varieties difficult.

The introduction of new varieties helped to increase the Victorian interest in ivies, their garden uses and cultivation, which is epitomised in that classic of the ivy world, Shirley Hibberd's *The Ivy*, published in 1872 with a second edition in 1893. *The Ivy*, now a rare item, exudes the prosy charm of that Victorian era. Hibberd, the son of a sea captain who had sailed under Nelson, was intended by his parents to become a doctor; he turned, however, to journalism, concentrating on horticulture and home decoration; in these fields in the late Victorian period he could hardly go wrong. He edited a periodical, 'Floral World', from 1858 until 1875, and in addition to *The Ivy* wrote such books as *Brambles and Bayleaves*, *Profitable Gardening* and *Familiar Garden Flowers*: all are now collectors' items. His writings convey the comfortable, well-ordered, quietly industrious life of the Victorian middle classes.

With lectures on ivies to the Royal Horticultural Society and other learned bodies, and his book and sundry writings on the subject, Hibberd became the international authority on ivy and the naming of its many varieties. Unfortunately in his book he ignored

14

the naming already carried out by William Paul – indeed he appeared to despise nurserymen somewhat, and this may have been the reason for his arbitrary replacement of Paul's names by his own. Whatever the reason it was the beginning of a confusion that grew over the years. His book was topical and drew attention to the merits of ivies but the genus could have had a better champion. First, he ignored the careful and well-argued definitions of the species of ivy made by the botanist Berthold Seeman (1864). This was the subject of argument between the two men in the columns of the 'Gardener's Chronicle' but the result was that the confusion over species, which was initiated by Hibberd, lasted almost fifty years. Secondly, he abhorred the use of personal names for varieties, for example the 'Cavendishii' of Paul, commemorating the Cavendish family. He replaced these with latinised names, transgressing the time-honoured rule that the name first given has priority. Some people adhered to the familiar names, others followed Hibberd and this kind of confusion has persisted to the present day. Thus the well-known 'Bird's Foot' ivy *H. helix* 'Caenwoodiana' which took its name from Caenwood House, a celebrated garden in Hampstead in the early 1800s, was re-named by Hibberd 'Pedata' and to this day we have two names in circulation for the same plant, a situation which the International Registration Authority will endeavour to resolve. Despite these criticisms anyone reading *The Ivy* must be struck by the wide sweep of the author's trawl. There can be no quotation that he has not included: Euripedes, Virgil, Cato, Horace, Dickens, Keats, Tennyson and many more are there. All the myth, magic and tradition of ivy he unearthed and presented, delicately and in a manner evocative of the age: the book in fact is a charming piece of Victoriana.

The period from 1872 onwards saw a proliferation of ivy varieties, or clones as many were, with firms like William Clibran & Son of Altrincham, Cheshire and Dicksons of Chester listing as many as fifty or sixty varieties. The Royal Horticultural Society maintained an ivy collection at its Chiswick gardens and conducted a trial comprising forty-six varieties. These were described in a report on the trial by Hibberd in the Society's journal and given awards according to their garden value. Interest in the cultivation of ivies rose to a peak in this period which ended, as did so many things, on 4 August 1914.

After World War 1 and during the 1920s horticultural interest in ivies declined. Anything associated with the Victorian–Edwardian era was out of fashion and nurserymen listed fewer and fewer varieties. Despite this there occurred in America a development that was to have a marked effect on the future of cultivated ivies. In the early 1920s Mr Paul Randolph of Verona, Pennsylvania, noticed a sport (or mutation) in a plant among a batch of common ivy; the mutation differed in having smaller, thinner leaves and a very branching habit; that is, it tended to produce sideshoots at almost every node. Mr Randolph put this into commerce as 'Pittsburgh'. A new race of ivies had arisen; from then into the 1930s further mutations occurred and by 1940 Bates, writing in the 'American National Horticultural Magazine', could describe eleven new varieties or clones. In the course of trade these spread to Europe, to Holland and Germany in particular, slowly gaining favour until World War 2 checked frivolities of this kind. With the return of peace, contacts with Europe introduced to British homes the fashion for house plants. This development was pioneered in Britain by Thomas Rochford Ltd., who steadily turned their vast tomato nurseries over to pot-plant production among which those most suitable of all house plants, ivies, were produced by the million.

Numerous nurseries followed this trend, obtaining their stock plants from many sources. The original names were not always available; nurseries often exchanged material and for various reasons did not always know the name of the plant they were propagating; they gave it what seemed an appropriate name and so more confusion was built upon that created by Hibberd a hundred years earlier.

Yet one further source of confusion conspires: Hederas are prone to variation and are propagated vegetatively by cuttings. A form with a particular colour or leaf will invariably throw shoots here and there that are a little 'offbeat' with perhaps larger leaves or less colour. If cuttings are taken haphazardly, perhaps under pressure of work or by unskilled labour, variation in the stock will arise and gradually that nursery's stock of a variety can acquire a markedly different character. This has happened noticeably in 'Glacier', 'Pittsburgh' and 'Königer's Auslese', clones that have been propagated in vast numbers in many very different nurseries.

These sources of confusion have produced many instances of several names being applied to one variety or clone. This may not seem important but in fact it can cause much frustration to those seeking a particular variety and can mean financial loss to nurserymen who unwittingly supply plants that are not the variety the customer had in mind. In this book it will be seen that considerable attention is given to defining the correct name and giving an accurate description.

This confusion over names should not arise in future, for in 1954 the International Code of Nomenclature for Cultivated Plants, which had been prepared by the International Committee on Horticultural Nomenclature and Registration, was agreed. In operating the Code the Authority has at times allocated genera which have particularly complex nomenclatural problems to specialist societies where these exist. Thus the nomenclature of rhododendron cultivars was entrusted to the Royal Horticultural Society whose experience and records go back many years. The USA has a flourishing Ivy Society and has shown great initiative in ivy matters; accordingly the International Authority appointed it as the world-wide registration body for ivy nomenclature. This means that any new name given to an ivy clone should be registered with, and accepted by, the Society's Registrar who can reject names already given to another variety, names which may be easily confused with others, or names that do not comply with the International Rules of Nomenclature. The Society is American-based but readily accepts overseas members. It publishes an informal Bulletin on ivy matters four times a year which should be perused by anyone seriously interested in ivies. Its address is The American Ivy Society, National Center for American Horticulture, Mt Vernon, Virginia, 22121, USA.

Nomenclature

The world's plant life is divided by botanists into divisions, classes and orders and then into families within which are genera. Systematic or taxonomic botany, the section of botanical study that classifies plants, is based primarily on the similarities of the floral parts of one plant with those of another so that all genera within a family bear a close resemblance to one another in this respect, and, while leaves and the plant's habit can vary considerably, the floral similarities are consistent. The members of a genus are termed species. All members of a genus bear the name of that genus: all ivies, for example, are of the genus *Hedera*, while each species has its own distinctive name; thus we have *Hedera helix*, the common ivy, or *Hedera colchica*, the Persian ivy.

Before the work of the Swedish botanist Linnaeus (1707–78) 'father' of systematic botany, plants had been named by multiple-worded Latin descriptions. Linnaeus brought order into this chaos by his institution of the binomial, or two-name system. It was Linnaeus in his *Species Plantarum* (1753) who defined the ivy's generic name as *Hedera*, using the old Latin name, and for the specific name he used the *helix* which Pliny had used for the climbing plant he knew. The Italian common name 'Edera' and the Spanish 'Hiedra' show a link with the past. The French name is 'Lierre', the Russian 'Bljustach', the German 'Epheu', cognate with English 'ivy', and the Dutch 'Klimop', appropriate to English ears, and indeed meaning 'climbing up'. It is possible that the common name 'ivy' derives from Latin 'ibex' meaning 'climber'.

There is sometimes variation within species and botanists allow for this by sub-division into categories called sub-species, varietas or forma. These botanical categories are normally reserved for morphological or geographical variants of a species. An ivy example is *Hedera helix* var. poetica, a yellow/orange fruited variant of the common ivy found in S.E. Europe and the Caucasus.

In addition to botanical variants, horticulturists over the years have selected individual plants from the wild. These have been named and propagated and are called cultivars (abr. cv). An ivy example is the tooth-leaved form of *Hedera colchica* known as 'Dentata'. A somewhat different example is the Irish Ivy, *Hedera helix* 'Hibernica'. This is a tetraploid having its chromosomes arranged in a manner different from that of the common ivy resulting in greater vigour and leafage.

Most cultivated ivies are in fact 'clones', a category of cultivar distinguished by its genetic uniformity and derived by vegetative propagation from a single individual. Such a clone will have been raised originally from a stem that 'sported' or mutated, undergoing some change in the arrangement of the cells governing colour or form. In nature this change would not persist unless it was to the plant's advantage, and increased its ability to grow, to obtain more sunlight or more ground space in the competitive world of nature. Few of the changes that make ivies interesting to horticulturists are useful to the plant, and they would normally die out by being overtaken by the usual and more useful growth. Mutations, however, are noted by keen gardeners; cuttings taken and with subsequent propagation a uniform plant population is built up and the introduction given a name. Nowadays these must be factual names and not in Latin form although latinised epithets such as 'Dentata' if published before 1 January 1959 are valid and indeed must not be replaced.

Sometimes very similar clones of different origins occur, and these may be difficult to distinguish accurately from one another. In order to prevent the confusion which would arise by naming each of these clones separately it is permissible under the Cultivated Plant Code to provide a group name. An example is *Hedera helix* group, which covers a number of very similar clones. The use of the term 'group' indicates that the name does not cover a single stable clone, and that slight variation may occur. Of course, if an individual clone in the group can be distinguished then a separate clonal name may be given.

Many ivies, certainly all the climbing kinds, can develop two kinds of leaf growth – juvenile and adult. The majority of plants, although they may begin life with a cotyledon leaf that differs from the ultimate true leaves, maintain a consistent leaf type once they have left the seedling stage. A few genera, however, have some species whose leaves take on different shapes at different stages of their existence, a phenomenon known as dimorphism; *Hedera* is

one of these. When some *Hedera* species achieve a measure of eleva-
tion and maturity the upper leaves lose their typically lobed outline
and become elliptical in shape. The plant then throws out stems
and the familiar flowering shoots that in the autumn are so attractive to flies, late wasps and a few bees. The reasons for dimorphism
are not fully understood as yet but it would seem reasonable to
assume that a lobed leaf may be more efficient in catching the
precious sunlight necessary to photosynthesis; it would be a useful
adaptation for a plant creeping along the forest floor until it can
ascend to better light where it finds the sunlight and air necessary
to flower, safe in the possession of a better environment for attract-
ing the flies upon which the fertilisation of its autumnal flowers
depends. The long and complex course of evolution may also have
decreed that having achieved sun and air a narrow unlobed leaf
is better adapted to survive any drought conditions that may occur
than a wide-lobed leaf.

Much of this is speculation; for the practical gardener the fact
remains that usually the juvenile leaves are the more attractive.
The plant's dimorphic habit has a bonus, however: if cuttings are
taken from the flowering shoots they retain the adult leaf character
and the arborescent habit; they remain in fact 'Tree Ivies' and can
grow into substantial self-supporting bushes up to 6 ft (1.8 m) high.
In most of the nineteenth-century ivy literature, and indeed in
many modern reference books, Tree Ivies are given an additional
Latin name, usually *arborea* or *arborescens*. I have made no
attempt to do this because in fact, with care and good propagating
facilities, the adult shoots from any climbing-type ivy may be made
to root and produce a tree form so that one could apply the term
'arborescens' to all the climbing ivies. The production of Tree Ivies
is a tribute to the propagator's art in the same way that a Standard
Ivy is a product of the grafter's expertise.

The habit of dimorphism, the production of adult leaves and
flowering shoots, is confined to the climbing or 'vining' types of
ivy. The self-branching ivies which throw shoots from almost every
node and tend to remain bushy or to climb very slowly are, in my
experience, non-flowering and do not produce adult leaves. The
self-branching ivies, 'ramulose' as Bates the American horticultural
writer called them, originated in America. They are valuable to
the horticulturist and interesting in that the possibility exists that

ivies non-indigenous to North America have mutated more in their new environment than in their native habitat. A similar situation has been noted in conifers – those from North America when introduced to Europe have produced more variations in leaf and form than has been the case in their native America.

The ivy is a plant of the Old World with a distribution extending from Japan in the east to the Azores in the west and from northern Europe to north Africa. Botanists are generally agreed in defining six species: geographically from east to west are *Hedera rhombea*, native to Japan and Korea; *H. nepalensis* from the Himalayas; *H. colchica*, south of the Caspian and west to Turkey; *H. pastuchovii*, similar distribution to *colchica*; *Hedera helix*, native to Europe as far north as southern Scandinavia, west to Britain and east to western Russia and south to the Caucasus; finally *Hedera canariensis* native to the Canary Islands, Madeira, the Azores, Portugal and north-west Africa to Algeria. The plant is not naturally present in the Americas or Australasia.

The German botanist Tobler (1912) suggested that the ivy probably originated in the Himalayan region and spread westwards. If Tobler's theory is correct the older species would be *rhombea*, *nepalensis* and *colchica*. This seems likely for these species appear to be more stable, showing few tendencies to vary in any respect, whereas *helix*, the newcomer, is extremely variable in leaf form and habit. There is evidence of linking forms between *colchica* and *helix* in Russia and more recently of intermediate forms in Spain and north Africa. Early botanists put many different plants into the *Hedera* genus including the Virginia Creeper. Credit belongs to Dr Berthold Seeman who in 1864 in the 'Journal of Botany' published his detailed revision of the family *Araliaceae*, or *Hederaceae* as it was then called, to which *Hedera* belongs. Seeman came from Germany to enter the Royal Botanic Gardens at Kew as a student gardener and stayed in Britain to become an eminent botanist. He defined three main species: *helix*, *canariensis* and *colchica*. This revision, although largely ignored by Hibberd (1872), has endured and, with additions, is accepted to this day. Recent years have seen a revival of interest in the ivy and a comprehensive botanical review of the species would be welcome. In this book the horticultural use of ivies is considered, with the house and garden use of its many variants.

Ivies for House, Garden and Landscape

For more than a century, writers and landscape gardeners have stressed the usefulness of ivy in garden design, yet it is still doubtful whether full advantage is taken of this most accommodating of climbing plants.

Ivies are remarkably adaptable, but generally do best on alkaline soils. Garden or house walls often provide this by the lime or mortar in their foundations. If the support is not a wall or the planting is for ground cover or rockwork and the soil is acid, it is a good plan to add lime in some form, preferably old mortar rubble or crushed chalk. This should not be done if the border is designed to receive acid-loving plants such as heathers or rhododendrons; most ivies will tolerate the acid soil and still grow well enough.

Planting should be as for other shrubs or climbers with a hole dug out somewhat larger than the root-ball of the plant, the roots gently spread in the hole with the neck of the plant at soil surface level, the hole filled and the soil firmed around the roots. Spring and autumn are the best planting seasons, but pot-grown ivies can be planted at any time. In dry conditions the planting hole should be filled with water prior to planting and care taken to ensure that the plant does not dry out in its early days. Plants for wall coverage should be planted as near to the wall as is practicable with the leading shoot directed to it. If the shoot is long it may be fixed with loose ties to wall-nails or similar fixing. Given this gentle guidance the climbing characteristics of the ivy will soon take over.

It should be emphasised that ivy is primarily a woodland plant, preferring light shade. As a house plant a temperature of 45–60°F (7–16°C) suits it very well; pot-plant producers often grow at higher temperatures to get rapid build up and more batches through their production lines. One may sometimes see ivies in windows in full sun, dry and with temperatures above 80°F (27°C).

This will not kill them but they will become hard in growth and un-typical, the leaves turning red or purple under stress, and prone to mite attacks. Light shade, moderate temperatures and moisture are the secrets of indoor ivy success.

House and Garden Walls and Background Planting

It is a fact, though often disputed, that ivies will not harm any building that is in good repair. The museum buildings at the Royal Botanic Gardens, Kew, Surrey, have supported ivies for almost one hundred years with no sign of trouble, and old buildings covered with ivy often retain a freedom from damp which they would lose if deprived of their leafy insulation.

Vigorous *helix* ivies that have reached the top of walls or houses benefit from a biennial or sometimes annual clip with shears to remove old leaves and insect harbourage. This is best done in early spring and before, of course, birds have had an opportunity to build nests; the plant will rapidly cover itself with fresh growth. This clipping is not necessary for *colchica* types or *nepalensis* unless they have outgrown their situation when they are best pruned back with secateurs. Clipping is likely to be necessary for *canariensis* types only after a severe winter that has scorched and browned the leaves. Ivies will grow on south-facing walls but are very much more suitable for north, east or west aspects. In any event south-facing walls are best reserved for climbers needing the sun's warmth.

When considering varieties suitable for house-cover, leaf size, shape and colour must be borne in mind. The large-leaved varieties such as *colchica* 'Dentata' and *helix* 'Hibernica' are admirable for large houses or large wall expanses. For smaller areas it is better to plant smaller-leaved varieties or clones such as 'Deltoidea' with its interesting shield-shaped leaves, while 'Pedata', the Bird's Foot ivy, makes a contrast to the broader-leaved kinds by its distinctive leaf shape. The variegated 'Cavendishii' looks well against red brick as does 'Buttercup' with leaves of lime-green to yellow; 'Atropurpurea' or 'Glymii' with their purple winger leaves look best against white or stone walls.

If there are borders in front of the wall against which ivy is grown, consideration should be given both to the ivy and the plants that may grow in front of it. For example, 'Buttercup' with a front

23

planting of cultivars of the blue shrub *Caryopteris* or blue-flowered *Ceratostigma* makes a splendid picture. Alternatively, a blue clematis such as 'Perle d'Azure' may be planted to scramble over it making the same colour contrast. The winter leafage and stems of the clematis may be cut well down to reveal the winter lime-green of the ivy; 'Buttercup' also makes a superb backing for purple-leaved shrubs such as *Cotinus coggygria* 'Notcutt's Variety' or the cultivar 'Kromhout'.

The purple ivies, 'Atropurpurea' or 'Glymii' make good back-grounds for grey-leaved shrubs such as *Senecio laxifolius* or the yellow-berried cultivars of pyracantha. Another attractive combination is made by 'Glacier' climbing up through *Cotoneaster horizontalis*. The silvery grey-green leaves make a lovely foil for the red berries. *Hedera canariensis* 'Gloire de Marengo' is a climber for fairly large walls and can turn an unattractive house wall into a feature; not as hardy as *helix*, one must be prepared, in Britain and other temperature areas, for some leaf damage in severe winters. For any area of wall above about 8 sq ft (2.5 sq m) there is the superb, hardy, brightly variegated *colchica* 'Dentata Variegata', probably the best variegated climbing plant in existence. It is challenged only by the splendid *helix* clone 'Goldheart'. This is suitable for both large and small walls, though on bigger walls when it is still growing upwards it seems to retain its glorious colour combination of green and yellow better than on small walls. Any green reverted shoots should be cut out as soon as they appear.

The Himalayan Ivy, *H. nepalensis* is a fine plant for a north wall. The leaves have a distinctive 'stepped' outline and hang so as to give a neat effect almost like a tile-hung wall. The slightly rusty stem colour and the olive-green leaves make a good backcloth for plants such as mauve or blue Michaelmas daisies (*Aster* cultivars) or orange-yellow flowers such as heleniums or crocosmia.

The soft grey-cream of 'Sulphurea' makes it an ideal background for scarlet or blue flowers such as phlox, red roses or delphiniums. If climbing red roses are a favourite, but only a red-brick wall where they would not show to advantage is available one can interpose a curtain of 'Sulphurea' on the wall, a pleasant sight in winter and an admirable background for the roses. In the same way *Clematis jackmanii*, lovely against a white wall, loses much of its attraction when seen against red brick; if allowed to climb up against an ivy such as 'Glacier' or 'Sulphurea' the deep purple flowers show to advantage.

The variegated and coloured ivies should not be clipped unless they are outgrowing their situation.

Cover for Sheds, Garages and other Buildings

One assumes that house and garden walls have at least some architectural merit, but this is not always so with garages or garden sheds. A quick-growing evergreen climber is often needed and nothing excels ivy for this purpose. Obtrusive concrete, cheap brick or asbestos can become most attractive with that 'Old World' air that ivy can bestow.

For a fairly large building few varieties equal the quick-growing, vigorous *helix* 'Hibernica'; it is worth obtaining the variegated clone, hardly less vigorous than the type and although mostly throwing green-leaved shoots, it occasionally throws shoots with striking cream-yellow variegation. The bright-green leaves of 'Angularis' make it another suitable variety for the purpose and having smaller leaves it is better for small buildings. Here again it is worth planting the clone 'Angularis Aurea' which has suffused yellow colouring to some of the leaves. The striking variegation of *colchica* 'Dentata Variegata' will convert the most mundane building into a garden feature to which the eye will be drawn. This should be considered when planting, for if it is better that the building be camouflaged and melt into the background one should plant 'Hibernica' or 'Angularis'. The varieties 'Digitata' and 'Triloba' are quick growing, pleasantly green and suitable for the same purpose.

Ivies for shed covering will not necessarily need the clipping suggested for ivies on walls. When the ivy reaches the roof it will bush out with adult growth. Generally it is best to let well alone, cutting away growth only where it might interfere with the use of the shed or building.

Ground Cover

The term 'Ground Cover' is applied to plants which by their spreading and close habit of growth cover the ground to the exclusion of weeds. It must be emphasised that although ground cover may restrict perennial weeds it seldom eliminates them. Areas proposed for planting should be free of perennial weed. The cover will preclude annual weeds and when thick, the seed-borne establishment of perennial weeds. Ivies are very suitable plants for ground cover and increasingly used in these days of high-cost garden labour. The idea is not new: ivy-clad banks and beds were often a feature of large gardens in Victorian times. Interestingly M. Delchevalerie, Chef de Culture au Fleuriste of the City of Paris, writing in *La Belgique Horticole* in 1868 recommended 'Le Lierre d'Irland' – *H. helix* 'Hibernica' – for this purpose in towns. His advice was indeed followed as can be seen in Paris and many other European cities.

The characteristics required of ground-cover ivies are close leafage, a spreading habit, resistance to frost and general toughness. There are not many varieties and clones that fulfil all these requirements, although a walk through almost any wood in Britain and northern Europe shows the suitability of the common ivy, *Hedera helix*, for the purpose. There are, however, better kinds for garden situations. First is that mentioned by M. Delchevalerie, namely 'Hibernica'. Seldom affected by frost on the continent of Europe and in Britain and extensively grown in America, its slightly fluted, somewhat matt-green leaves are close enough to make good cover while its vigour ensures spread. Tolerant of town conditions and shade it has been used to hide many an eyesore.

For reasonably large areas the striking Elephant's Ears of *Hedera colchica* 'Dentata' make interesting and effective ground cover. The plant runs more widely but less thickly than 'Hibernica' and needs rather better soil. It is frost hardy as is its variegated clone 'Dentata Variegata' which will bring light to any dull corner. The species itself, *H. colchica*, is less suitable because of its smaller leaves and care should be taken not to purchase it in error. Another hardy ground-cover ivy is 'Sulphurea'; grey-green and soft cream, its leafage is not quite as thick as the previous examples but is suitable and appropriate for smaller areas. Other *helix* clones for such positions are 'Parsley Crested', 'Manda's Crested' and 'Königer's Auslese'. All have proved more frost resistant than might be expected and by the variation of their foliage make interesting ground-cover contrasts.

Areas which do not have severe winter frosts or searing winds have a wider choice. They can use the lush, leafy *canariensis* clones such as the silver variegated 'Gloire de Marengo' or 'Striata' with its slight gold marking in the leaf centre, *Hedera canariensis* itself or its broad-leaved variant 'Ravensholst'.

Planting distances are governed by the speed with which cover is demanded. One plant of 'Hibernica' will cover about 10 sq yd (9 sq m) in three or four years. Most people, particularly landscape architects and parks departments, need cover more rapidly, and for this plants should be set out at 2 ft (60 cm) squares. The plants are usually pot grown but some enterprising nurserymen make use of the 'Nisula' roll technique as used in raising forest tree transplants. Rooted cuttings are laid on a length of black polythene about 1 ft (30 cm) wide. A thin layer of peat/sand compost is laid on the cuttings whose 'collars' are about 2 in (5 cm) below the top edge of the strip and whose leaves consequently extend outside the area of plastic. The strip is rolled up and the end fixed with a clip. Stood on a concrete standing area the roll now appears as a large plastic pot packed with concentric rings of cuttings. The rolls are watered and attended as if they were pots and when growth has been made, sold according to the numbers contained which may be twenty-five to fifty. The advantage for landscape architects or parks departments is ease of transport: plants may be planted in a spade 'nick' instead of being trowelled as for pots and there are no pots to clear away. For planting large areas the economy is worthwhile.

Rock Gardens

Rock gardens tend to be planted in one of two main styles. The first is after the tradition of Reginald Farrer, as a garden of alpine flowers based on nature's own rock gardens and providing suitable habitats for true alpine plants. The other could be termed public or municipal, where attractive and often very natural rock and water effects, although planted primarily with alpines, are filled in with various non-alpines to provide colour and display for as long as possible.

For the first kind of rock garden probably the only ivies to be admitted are the small-leaved clones of *helix* that make ground cover for small bulbs, particularly those such as early crocus species or the delicate flowers of *Leucojum autumnale* that benefit from protection from mud-splash. Small-leaved ivies such as 'Walthamensis', 'Prof. Friedrich Tobler' or the minute 'Spetchley' are excellent for this purpose. Three ivies, *H. helix* 'Conglomerata', 'Erecta' and 'Congesta' are often seen on rock gardens, even those of the alpine purist; 'Conglomerata' will cover a rock attractively with its stubby stems and wavy leaves while the erect, self-supporting stems of 'Erecta' and 'Congesta', the latter of finer growth and narrower leaves, are very effective as spot plants.

While the purist's rock garden would not, indeed should not, admit variegated ivies, the more showy 'public' type of garden need have no such inhibitions. On big rock gardens backgrounds may be needed or a drift of evergreen to link the rock garden into surrounding features. For these purposes few ivies can equal *H. colchica* 'Sulphur Heart', large-leaved and with enough variegation to provide interest but not flamboyance. On rocks or alpine pockets the small variegated clones such as 'Eva', 'Harald' and 'Sagittifolia Variegata' provide colour and a good background to bright-coloured annuals or flowering bulbs. The glossy green 'Ivalace' with its distinct crimpled leaves can be used for this purpose or to climb or hang over rocks.

House Plants

The virtue of ivies as house plants is now well established and is a welcome swing of the pendulum of fashion. Their suitability for cultivation indoors, in pots, glass cases or special window cases, was recognised in Britain and Europe in Victorian times. The modern house-plant trade, however, has a far greater range of varieties available for the purpose. Much of this is due to the American interest in ivies between the wars which resulted in the introduction of 'Pittsburgh' and other self-branching kinds. These were introduced to Europe and after World War 2 were produced in vast quantities. Given the variable nature of *Hedera helix* these large numbers gave a higher chance, by natural mutations, of the emergence of new varieties, an opportunity embraced with enthusiasm on both sides of the Atlantic.

House-plant ivies sold as pot plants are often produced by inserting three to five rooted cuttings to a 5 in (12 cm) pot. The pot-grown ivy is a good house plant in its own right; alternatively, several different varieties may be planted in plant troughs. Short-jointed kinds such as 'Eva', 'Harald', 'Luzii', 'Glacier', 'Stift Neuburg', 'Ivalace', 'Green Feather' and 'Merion Beauty' are suitable. If required as a room divider the trough may be set against a lattice screen of wood or metal and the plants set to climb it. Varieties of a climbing habit are necessary: *H. canariensis* 'Gloire de Marengo', 'Cavendishii', 'Manda's Crested' and 'Green Ripple' may be tried in this situation. Because of its comparative permanence the lattice must be in a reasonably good light situation; poor light can lead to pale, attenuated growth.

There are many new clones whose unusual leaf shapes and variegation show to good effect as pot plants. In addition to those mentioned above the following are some of the more noteworthy: 'Ardingly', 'Big Deal', 'Boskoop', 'Bruder Ingobert', 'Cockle Shell', 'Domino', Fantasia', 'Fluffy Ruffles', 'Kolibri', 'Kurios', 'Old Lace', 'Sinclair Silverleaf', 'Small Deal', 'Trinity', 'Triton', 'Williamsiana' and 'Zebra'.

Pillar Ivies

Elegant ivy pillars, suitable as decorative features in the home and also for large displays in hotel foyers and the like, may be built around moss-sticks. Previously these were based on bamboo canes but nowadays rigid plastic tubing of the kind used for water pipes is used. The length may vary from 3–6 ft (0.9–1.8 m) according to requirements and the diameter should be about $1\frac{1}{2}$ in (4 cm). Sphagnum moss is bound with twine around the pipe so that it is encased in a coat of moss. The stick is then plunged in the compost-filled pot, 6–10 in (15–25 cm) in diameter according to the stick length. One or two ivies are planted and trained, preferably in a twisting fashion, up the moss-stick which they eventually clothe completely. The stick should be kept moist and indeed a fairly warm and moist growing atmosphere is best to get the plants going.

A variation on this is the familiar pyramid made by inserting three or four canes down the sides of a compost-filled pot and tying the cane tips at the top; hoops of stout wire can also be used. All these erect types of support require climbing kinds of ivy. The following have been used with success: *H. canariensis* 'Gloire de

Marengo' and 'Margino-maculata', and the *helix* clones, 'Green Feather', 'Shamrock', 'Glacier', 'Parsley Crested' and 'Green Ripple'. 'Goldheart' may be used but needs to be grown up quickly. Of them all 'Gloire de Marengo' is the most widely used and from the number grown one would imagine it to be in every house, office and public building throughout the ivy-growing world. It is popular, a good-tempered plant for the purpose and with bright variegation.

Hanging Baskets

These are an interesting form of floral decoration for verandas and patios and often a cherished feature where they occur. For good effect they require brightly coloured flowers but these do not always trail and hang down as quickly as required. Small-leaved ivies can fulfil this purpose very well. Grown in house or greenhouse in 3–4 in (8–10 cm) pots, and then planted three or four to a basket they hang down giving pleasant backing to pelargoniums and fuchsias until lobelia, lysimachia or similar flowering plants trail and blend their flowers with the ivy. It is possible, of course, to make an all-ivy hanging basket, supplementing the trailing kinds with short-jointed, variegated kinds for the centre of the basket. The clone Professor Friedrich Tobler' is unsurpassed for hanging baskets: its deeply split foliage is most unusual and readily provokes comment and query. For the centres, clones such as 'Ardingly', 'Williamsiana', 'Luzii' and 'Eva' are very suitable.

Topiary

At present the charming fashion of ivy topiary seems peculiar to America, although there is evidence that the Victorian Britons trained their ivy in this fashion. Perhaps this brief description will encourage its wider use. Wire topiary forms are sold, fashioned as animals, birds, cones, umbrellas and globes and could indeed be made in almost any shape one can imagine. The chosen form is stuffed with moss, which has been soaked in a dilute fertiliser solution, then planted with a number of rooted cuttings of suitable short-jointed clones such as 'Ivalace', 'Shamrock', 'Glacier', 'Eva' or 'Green Feather'. The moss is watered as required with water containing a slight boost of a balanced liquid fertiliser. Frequent overhead water sprays, with a fine-rose can or a hand-held spray, keep the moss moist and help deter mites. The plants will have been planted at regular intervals and fairly closely over the topiary form. As they grow the sideshoots are pinched and trimmed so as to produce eventually an ivy-clad figure on the basis of the chosen form.

Suitable wire forms are on sale in the USA and doubtless if demand arises will soon appear in Europe. Failing this the enthusiast can contrive his own, and indeed with skill and dedication can produce a form depicting his favourite pet or interest.

Bottle Gardens and Terraria

The fact that a virtually enclosed glass vessel will support plant life for long periods with minimum attention has been known for well over a century. The principle was used in the form of the botanical 'Wardian Case' extensively used for the long-distance conveyance of plants before the advent of rapid air transport. The present vogue for bottle gardens makes use of the same principle. Broad-based glass bottles of some 12 in (30 cm) diameter at the base and about the same height taper to a 3 in (8 cm) open neck. A layer of moist soilless compost is placed in the bottom and, using long tweezers or tongs, three or four plants of a suitable selection are planted in the compost and lightly watered in. Plants often used are the smaller dracaenas, cryptanthus, leaf begonias and of course *Hedera*, usually a variegated clone such as 'Harald'. Leaving aside the other plants it is possible to make a very attractive bottle garden with the same technique but using only Hederas. Suitable clones are 'Harald', 'Kolibri', 'Stift Neuburg', 'Bruder Ingobert', 'Ardingly', 'Spetchley', 'Williamsiana', 'Eva', 'Cockle Shell' and 'Adam'. As with all bottle gardens, overcrowding problems will arise, initially controlled by careful trimming but finally requiring a re-plant.

Terraria are glass cases similar to household aquariums and, indeed, like the original Wardian case. Planting and growing techniques are the same as for bottle gardens but as the top is open, or has a removable lid, access is easier and a more extensive range can be grown.

Landscape Gardening

In his book *The Ivy* (1872) Shirley Hibberd, the Victorian garden writer, explains how pot-grown specimens of 'Tree Ivies' and 'Standard Ivies' may be used as winter bedding. The increasing cost of traditional winter bedding plants such as wallflowers and tulips may yet lead to a revival of this practice.

To raise Tree Ivies, cuttings from shoots that have assumed the adult phase are taken and when rooted, potted on into larger pots, until they are suitable for 9 in (23 cm) pots. A cane or stake will initially be necessary to prevent untidy growth. In three years a reasonable pot shrub will result which can be bedded out as Hibberd suggested or used in other landscape effects.

Height and interest can be further achieved by using Standard Ivies. These can be produced by grafting shoots of a chosen clone on to stems of × *Fatshedera lizei*, the bi-generic hybrid (*Fatsia* × *Hedera*) which is easily raised from cuttings. These should have been pot grown and run up as single stems to the required height of 2–4 ft (0.6–1.2 m). Grafting, using a rind or crown graft with several grafts, should be done in a greenhouse. A warm, minimum 60°F (16°C), temperature and moist atmosphere will aid successful union.

The method of producing Standard Ivies advocated by Hibberd is, however, probably easier. Strong-rooted cuttings of the chosen clone are potted in a good compost and the shoot trained to a stick or cane; any sideshoots that appear are rubbed out until the required height is reached; it is then stopped and a few buds below the cut-off point allowed to develop to produce the necessary head. As the plants make more root they may be potted on, eventually into a 9 in (23 cm) pot when they may be used for winter bedding, plant and pot being sunk in the ground; like standard roses each will require a stake for support. They can of course make attractive items for indoor or greenhouse decoration.

In contrast to Victorian bedding schemes the formal areas around modern office developments, sports stadia, shopping precincts and the like require low maintenance-cost planting. Ground-cover plants are widely used with more prickly subjects such as *Berberis* and *Mahonia* for areas where trespass might be a temptation. For large areas, particularly in shady spots between buildings, imaginative planting of ivy can produce very satisfying results. A mass planting of 'Hibernica' can have among it spot plants of arborescent 'Dentata Variegata'. This pattern can be reversed, particularly if a shady corner needs to be lightened, by close planting juvenile 'Dentata Variegata' or 'Sulphur Heart' with spot plants of arborescent 'Hibernica'. Plants of 'Erecta' or 'Congesta' can be used as effect plants, for example at each side of the base of a flight of garden steps or as spot plants in fairly small beds with an underplanting of a variegated ivy such as 'Sulphurea'. A landscape effect with ivies that harks back to a more leisured era is the 'wall' made of Tree Ivies, closely planted. A most striking example of this is that surrounding the terrace at Kew Gardens, Surrey, upon which the great Palm House stands. Many people assume it to be an ivy-covered low wall but it is in fact a low clipped hedge of 'Hibernica'.

A fedge is defined as a cross between a fence and a hedge. It can be a useful feature and usually implies climbing plants on a fence of wire, wattle hurdle, spaced board or chestnut fencing. Climbing Ivies are excellent for the purpose. Initially they may need a little tying in as an encouragement to climb but kinds such as 'Deltoidea', 'Sulphurea', 'Digitata' or 'Palmata' quickly provide an evergreen face to what may have been an uninviting prospect. In similar fashion Victorian gardening books often show ivy-covered arbours; a sitting place of fairly rough and basic wood outline can become attractive when covered with ivy. On both fedge and arbour, clipping may be necessary and care taken to check adult growth which may bush out at the top and make the structure top-heavy.

Cultivation

Propagation

Most ivies are easy to propagate, producing trails which root at the nodes when lying on the soil. Sections of these trails when cut off often root easily and may be planted where they are required to grow, or, as a refinement, first planted in a frame of sandy soil.

For the commercial grower, or where large quantities are required, this method is hardly sufficient and in any event is not suitable for Tree Ivies or for *canariensis* or *colchica* varieties or non-trailing *helix* clones. For these, and for situations where quantities are required, the practice of taking nodal cuttings should be followed. These are made from trails or from the shoots available on bushy indoor ivies. They are sections of stem, cut so that the node is the base of the cutting which should have at least two leaves at or above the next node (see Diagram). In taking material it should be remembered that cuttings from adult shoots, that is, flowering shoots or shoots high up on a plant that has produced flowers, will produce Tree or Shrub Ivies; they are also more difficult to root.

Nodal cuttings may be inserted in a cold frame from October to November when the cuttings should be made about 5 in (12 cm) high and of the previous season's growth. Alternatively, cuttings made in July may be placed on a warm bench in a shaded glasshouse; they should be 3–4 in (7.5–10 cm) long and of semi-hard shoots. A sand/peat compost is suitable. The autumn cuttings are lifted and potted the following April, and summer cuttings after about six weeks.

The pot-plant trade depends on a full-looking pot of ivy, produced as quickly as possible in order to economise on heat and provide a quick turn-over. To this end five, six or seven small nodal cuttings are inserted in a 3 in (7.5 cm) pot filled with a normal potting compost, usually a sand/peat mix with nutrients. The pots are stood 'pot-thick', often under polythene tents within a glasshouse, and an average temperature of 65–70°F (18–21°C) maintained. The cuttings are kept moist by damping with watering can or spray. When rooted, the polythene is removed and the pots moved to a cooler house or the temperature is dropped to 60–65°F (15–18°C) for growing on. This method is effective with clones such as 'Ivalace', 'Harald' and 'Anna Marie'. *H. colchica* varieties take longer to root and do not respond readily to high temperatures. They are best rooted by nodal cuttings inserted in boxes or directly in sand beds on a mist bench in a glasshouse.

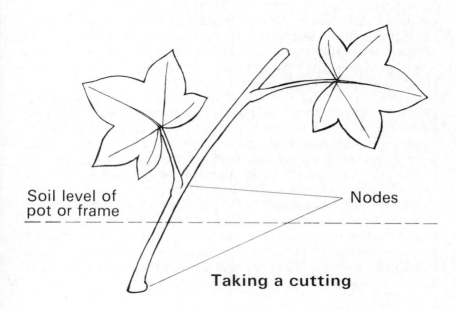

Soil level of
pot or frame

Nodes

Taking a cutting

When propagating clones that have a distinctive habit, leaf variegation or formation, care should be taken to use only material typical of the clone. The success of some nurseries in producing batches of good, acceptable plants, displaying the characteristics of the clone, is due mainly to care in selection of propagating material. The inclusion of only slightly off-type material can result in batches of uneven plants that are less acceptable to buyers and less easily identified as the clone that is being purchased.

Composts

Apart from topiary and outside planting, some form of compost is required for all other growing methods. In the past, potting soil was made using loam or garden soil, leaf-mould and sand, with the addition of bone-meal, sulphate of potash and lime according to the type of plant, while some growers favoured additions of organic materials bordering on the curious. Results were sometimes good but not consistently so. A few years prior to World War 2, W. J. C. Lawrence working at the John Innes Research Institute in England discovered that consistent growth and prevention of soil-borne diseases were effected by partial sterilisation of the loam, substitution of the leaf-mould by peat and the addition of small amounts of fertilisers. The resulting compost was called 'John Innes' and although devised for experimental work, became extensively used in commercial horticulture.

Loams vary however and, seeking an even more standardised growing medium, the University of California in the 1950s produced the 'U.C.' composts of peat, sand and balanced nutrients. These, with a few modifications, were widely adopted and although loam-based composts are still used for certain subjects the bulk of the pot plants produced in America, Britain and Europe are grown in peat/sand mixes. These are often produced under brand names but the constituents will normally be given on the bags. Ivies grow well in them but it must be remembered that the slow-release nutrients are used up as the plant grows and must be supplemented by liquid feeding. Remember also that once peat has dried out it is difficult to wet so plants in peat mixes should not be allowed to dry out completely.

Pests and Diseases

From the gardener's point of view one of the virtues of ivy is its ease of cultivation; whether outside or as a house plant it will survive treatment which would kill many other plants. In some respects this is unfortunate as it can result in plants either lingering in unsuitable soil and situations or being riddled with pests to which a lesser plant would have succumbed.

Soil for ivies growing outside should be reasonably open and supplied with organic material but not too rich in nitrogen, the leaf-forming nutrient supplied by fertilisers such as sulphate of ammonia. Too much nitrogen produces large soft leaves prone to disease attack. Organic material is necessary, for the ivy is essentially a woodland plant, doing well in humus-rich woodland conditions and although sometimes growing naturally in less-favourable situations, is at its best in chalk or limestone areas, a soil slightly on the alkaline side; a pH of about 7.5 to 8.5 suits it admirably.

PESTS

Ivy is a shade plant but one sometimes sees it planted on south-facing walls where it becomes a prey to mites who revel in such conditions. These pests are world-wide and will infest almost all plants. Most destructive is the Red Spider (or Two Spotted) Mite *Tetranychus urticae*. There are various biological types of this and of other mites but the kind of damage is common to all. It is first seen as a light yellow, fine spotting, commencing in small patches, but as the pest increases it covers the whole leaf. Sometimes the effect is not unlike the suffused variegation in clones such as 'Trinity' or 'Sinclair Silverleaf'. A check is easily made, however, by turning the leaf over and examining it closely, preferably with a hand-lens, when the yellowish mites, eight-legged and about 1 mm long are easily seen; in bad infestations the leaves may be covered with fine webbing among which the mites will actively move. The term 'Red Spider' refers to the resting stage and the brownish-red colour they assume when they lurk in crevices of plant tissue or glasshouse woodwork. They should not be confused with the harmless, larger, active scarlet spider, seen occasionally. The pest is encouraged by dry conditions.

Enemy Number Two for wall and house-plant ivies is undoubtedly scale. This, too, is a world-wide pest and includes Soft Scale *Coccus hesperidum*, Brown Scale *Eulecanium corni*, Oleander Scale *Aspidiotus hederae* and others. Often the first sign of the pest to the casual observer is a sooty deposit on some leaf surfaces. This in fact is a mould growing upon the sticky secretions made by the insects as they suck the plant-sap. These Scale insects have one common feature: the female is a round or flat, dark- to light-brown creature about 3–4 mm long adhering, usually, to the underside of the leaf. Beneath this shield the young scales are nurtured, eventually emerging as 'crawlers' who move to other leaves and settle; losing the power of movement they develop their protective covering and in turn produce more crawlers. They are most vulnerable to sprays when in this crawler stage. Some of the new insecticides are systemic in their action; that is, they are applied either as plant sprays or to the soil and are taken up in the sap flow. Mites (and aphids, too) sticking their mouthparts into the plant and sucking the sap receive a poisoned draught and cease operations. This type of insecticide is fairly long lasting and very effective but availability and regulations on use vary from country to country and may vary with future legislation.

Aphids – Greenfly, Blackfly, call them what you will – know no boundaries. Soft, sucking insects, the best known are probably Greenfly on roses and Blackfly on broad beans. In summer periods they produce living young parthenogenetically, that is without a sexual phase, and it is this rapidity of reproduction that makes them such a troublesome pest. As with Scale, it is often the presence of Sooty Mould on the leaf that is the first sign of their activity. On ivies they tend to colonise the young shoot-tips and can be a nuisance outside on 'Erecta' and similar types; seek advice for a good spray.

DISEASES

It is true to say that wall ivies are less troubled by fungal or bacterial troubles than are ground-cover or house-plant ivies, primarily because moist conditions predispose ivies on the ground or in pots to the fungal or bacterial troubles common, unhappily, to both America and Europe.

The presence of very black spots, often rather angular, on the leaves is symptomatic of Bacterial Leaf Spot *Xanthomonas hederae*. In Britain this is seen, fortunately not frequently, on glasshouse ivies and very rarely outside. Bacterial diseases are not easily controlled by sprays. If a rare or favoured plant is affected, picking off and immediately burning infected leaves may halt the spread, otherwise destruction of the plant by burning is the only course of action.

A more frequent trouble is Ivy Leaf Spot *Colletotrichum trichellum* or *Ameriosporium trichellum*. The symptoms are soft brown spots on the leaf, up to 1 cm diameter, in bad cases joining up to cause the collapse of the whole leaf. It is spread mainly by water splash and if ivies are grown in wet, humid conditions can become troublesome. It can be destructive outside, particularly on young growth in moist autumn periods. Fungicidal sprays to check this disease are often routine practice in commercial glasshouses. On a house or garden scale, preventive sprays may be worthwhile when the disease is seen and assuming the area of outside ground cover is small.

A less-common trouble is Black Leaf Spot *Phyllosticta hedericola*. In Britain this is infrequent, seen mainly on *Hedera colchica* and its clones, and seldom worth control measures. It can be unsightly and, if extensive, advice as to control spraying should be sought. The spots are large, 0.5–1.5 cm across, round, deep black and almost 'crusty' in appearance.

In Britain Powdery Mildew (*Oidium* sp.) has occasionally proved a problem under glass; strangely it affects only the glossy leaved form of *Hedera canariensis*. In the USA another mildew (*Erysiphe cichoracearum*) is reported but does not appear to be a problem.

Many plants propagated by vegetative means are plagued by virus problems but little is known of virus diseases in ivies. Virus particles have been isolated from some of the 'blotched' variegated ivies and in this respect they may be like other beneficial viruses that produce the mottled leaves of *Abutilon* 'Thomsonii' making it a useful bedding plant or the attractive yellow veining of *Lonicera japonica* 'Aureo-reticulata'. My research suggests that the clone *helix* 'Tesselata' which mysteriously ceased to exist a year or so after receiving an Award of Merit in 1893 was in fact a plant with a transient virus infection which produced a yellow veining similar to that in the *Lonicera*. Although impressive at the time, it did not persist. At present there do not appear to be any viruses having an adverse effect on ivies as ornamental plants.

CONTROL MEASURES

Advances in pest and disease control are rapid and continuous and specific recommendations made at the time of writing would easily be outdated by the time the book was read, or invalidated by the increasing legislation to which poisonous sprays are subject. Having identified the problem from the information given in this chapter it is easy to find the means for its control. In Britain there are plenty of sources for advice on up-to-date pesticides. The Royal Horticultural Society will advise its members and the general public can refer to County Horticultural Officers, Parks Departments, local Horticultural Societies or any reliable Horticultural Sundriesman. Similar sources exist in other countries and the USA, in addition to the University-based advisory organisation, has its own Ivy Society which gives specialised, locally based advice.

Descriptive Notes: Species, Varieties and Clones

The following list of species, varieties and clones aims to give information on origin, history and authenticity of name as well as characteristics of the ivy and notes on its ornamental value.

The parts of the plants, and the botanical and horticultural terms used, are shown in the glossary which follows the descriptions. Measurements of leaves are of average material in all cases and, it will be noted, are given in centimetres: metric measurements, just like Latin nomenclature, have helped to give botanists a common standard which surmounts language difficulties. References to American zones of plant hardiness can be checked against the map on page 163.

Leaf colour can be influenced by soil, situation, season or cultivation. The colours quoted are average, taken in late summer when growth is complete; in the case of indoor plants, from plants grown 'cool' and unforced. Books and catalogues often speak of 'gold' or 'silver' variegation but in fact these correspond to shades of yellow, white or cream to varying degrees. Thus a pronounced 'gold' is described here as yellow or perhaps yellow-cream if of a paler shade; 'silver' as white or possibly white-cream, the first colour mentioned being the predominant tone. In the same way greens are shown as dark, medium, light, grey-green or possibly green-grey. Stems are shown often as 'green-purple' or *vice versa* endeavouring to indicate the predominant tone.

Ivy is a variable plant and this has always made identification of varieties and clones difficult. It will be seen that emphasis has been placed on the determination and authenticity of the correct name; erroneous names which should be discarded are also indicated. In this way it is hoped that the descriptions will be of value, not only to the amateur gardener and those having charge of public gardens, but also to the nurserymen of those countries where the

41

sale and interest in ivies is increasing, and it becomes ever more essential for buyer and seller to know exactly what plant is meant by what name.

Not all the clones and varieties described in this book are commercially available, and if difficulty is experienced in obtaining any plant, enquiries can be directed to the American Ivy Society whose address is given at the end of the Introduction to this book.

Hedera canariensis

This plant, commonly called the Algerian, African or Canary Island ivy was named by the German botanist Willdenow in 1808, his type specimen being based on a collection made in the Canary Islands. The plant suffered a number of name changes. It was described as *algeriensis* (Hibberd, 1864); *maderensis* (Koch, 1869); *grandifolia* (Hibberd, 1872); *azorica* (Carrière, 1890); *sevillana* (Sprenger, 1903), and *canariensis* var. azorica (Bean, 1914). Seeman (1864) recognised the plant as *canariensis* but rather doubtfully linked it with the Irish Ivy *H. helix* 'Hibernica'. Lawrence & Schulze (1942) unravelled the tangle with a detailed description of the accepted *canariensis* of Willdenow, and Bean (1973) confirming *canariensis* as the plant we know today, draws attention to the confusion which existed during much of the nineteenth century between it and the Irish Ivy, 'Hibernica'. Catalogues of the period testify to this, so much so that it is often difficult to judge what plant they are listing.

Much of this confusion can be traced to Hibberd's reference (1872) to 'Irish ivy found in Portugal, the Canary Islands, Madeiras and the Iberian Peninsular' and his proposed name of *grandifolia* to cover both *canariensis* and 'Hibernica.'

Plants in circulation at the present time are often distributed as *Hedera* 'Monty' or 'Montgomery'. I can find no account of the origin of this name but the plant appears to be that described by Lawrence & Schulze. Also circulating as 'Monty' is a non-glossy, matt-leaved form with slightly broader leaves.

Recently it has been found that the glossy form of *canariensis* is, under glass in Britain, susceptible to powdery mildew (*Oidium* sp.) an unusual disease for ivies; this does not attack the matt-leaved form or any *helix* clones, however close together they are or whatever attempts are made to transfer the disease to them. This susceptibility must be due to some genetic weakness and may in the future assist in the determination of species among the north African ivies where recent research and collecting shows the existence of variations and possible new species.

For garden use *canariensis* is rather more hardy than its variegated clones 'Gloire de Marengo' or 'Striata'. Its virtues are rapid growth and glossy green foliage. It has recently found favour as a pot plant trained up moss-sticks in pyramid form.

Habit	Vining.
Stems	Red-green, smooth; hairs scale-like. 10–15 rays. Internodes 3–5 cm.
Petioles	Red-green, smooth.
Leaves	Unlobed, 10–15 cm by 8–12 cm, ovate, acuminate. Leaf base cordate, margin entire. Slight lobe-like protrusions on occasional leaves. Upper surface glossy, light green, rapidly darkening with age. Veins light green but not prominent.
	The matt-leaved clone is similar save for its dull-green surface, broader leaf, and more frequent occurrence of the lateral lobe-like protrusions; also for the fact that in cold weather the leaves turn purple more readily than the glossy clone.

'AZORICA'

Doubts have been raised by some botanists as to the correctness of this name, and understandably for the plant is completely unlike the smooth, glossy, red-stemmed ivy we associate with *canariensis*. No such doubts seem to have been in the mind of W. J. Bean (1914) who described it as 'A vigorous variety with leaves 3″ to 6″ across, vivid green, 5 or 7 lobed, lobes ovate, blunt pointed. The quite young wood and leaves are covered with a thick tawny felt. Introduced from St Michael in the Azores by the late firm of Osborn of Fulham.' This description is repeated in the 8th Edition (1973).

Osborn & Sons indeed listed an ivy as 'Azorica' in their catalogue as long ago as 1870 and presumably this was their introduction. Barr & Sons of London in 1895 listed it as 'Canariensis Azorica – Bright green, large foliage, rapid grower'. William Clibran & Sons of Altrincham, Cheshire catalogued it in 1894 as 'Hedera Azorica' and drew attention to the bluntly lobed foliage. A plant complying with all these descriptions and with Bean's more detailed analysis is still listed by a few nurserymen and is a climbing ivy of quiet character. In my experience it is not as hardy as *helix* but is slightly hardier than the species and its variegated forms. I have not found it as vigorous as did Bean and for this reason would hesitate to recommend it for ground cover. The *canariensis* clone 'Canary Cream' shares the green-stem character and may well be allied to this plant.

Habit	Vining.
Stems	Green. Internodes 3–4 cm.
Petioles	Green.
Leaves	Five to seven lobed, 9–11 cm by 10–12 cm. Centre lobe only slightly larger than the four laterals, the two additional lobes when present are little more than protrusions. Sinuses fairly shallow, lobes bluntly acute. Three to five rayed hairs are extensive on stem and leaf surfaces, persisting for some time on upper leaf surfaces and so extensive on stems and petioles as to give these a felted appearance. Colour bright mid-green, given a slight matt appearance by the abundant hairs, veins lighter. The plant shows no red coloration at all.

'GLOIRE DE MARENGO'

This variegated form of the African or Canary Island ivy is the most extensively grown house-plant ivy in Europe at the present time, as well as being extremely popular in America and elsewhere, but the history of its name is as confused as any.

Native to north Africa, the Azores, the Canaries and Madeira it was named *Hedera canariensis* by the German botanist Willdenow in 1808. The first record of a variegated form is that of Paul who in 1867 listed H. Algeriensis variegata, leaves green broadly margined with white, very large, growth rapid'. The last phrase is a vital clue since this is indeed the fastest-growing variegated ivy. Paul's classifications and descriptions were endorsed by the German botanist Karl Koch (1870) and the name came into general use. Confusion ensued when Hibberd (1872), in an attempt at

clarification named the African Ivy 'H. grandifolia' and its variegated form 'H. grandifolia "variegata"' but also incorporated
Hedera hibernica, the Irish Ivy, in synonomy. For the following
fifty years catalogues and writers variously used all three names
for what was certainly the same plant. Bean (1914) listed *H.
canariensis* with *H. algeriensis* and *H. maderensis* as synonyms but
made no mention of any variegated form; Rehder (1947) listed *H.
canariensis* as a 'related species' also making no mention of a variegated form. Lawrence & Schulze (1942) in their analysis of *H.
canariensis* 'cultivars' combined the 'H. Algeriensis "variegata"' of
Paul and the 'H. grandifolia "variegata"' of Hibberd as 'H.
canariensis "variegata"', conceding in a footnote that the plant had
been grown and distributed as 'Gloire de Marengo'. This was certainly true, for in 1924 Hillier & Sons of Winchester, Hampshire
listed '*Hedera canariensis variegata* "Gloire de Marengo"' while
Jackmans of Woking, Surrey in their *Planter's Handbook* for 1936
described it as '(having) large leaves, merging from green through
silvery-grey to silver at the edge', a description that is hard to fault.
The plant had therefore been in circulation as 'Gloire de Marengo'
for eighteen years prior to the Lawrence & Schulze analysis of 1942
and it seems unfortunate that they should have overlooked this
name in favour of a Latin specific: it must be remembered, however, that the year was 1942 and links with Europe were tenuous.

In 1927, W. Fromow, wholesale nurserymen of Windlesham,
Surrey, listed it as 'Souv. de Marengo' with no description; this
is a name still occasionally used and indeed revived by Krussman
(1977) who gives its origin as having been found at an Algerian
house 'Villa Marengo'. There is incidentally a small town named
'Marengo' near Mantua in Italy but I cannot trace any link with
the plant there. Despite Krussman's resurrection of this name
'Gloire de Marengo' is the valid name.

There appears to be only one form in existence apart from the
mottled 'Margino-maculata'. If 'Gloire de Marengo' was merely
an improved clone of a variegated form one would expect to find
situations with plants of the previous form which the better clone
had superseded. This is not so, and one must accept that 'Gloire
de Marengo' was a name which had appeal to the nursery trade
and the gardening public and has obviously stuck.

In summary it is suggested that this variegated form of the North

African ivy has been known for many years, certainly since 1867 when Paul described it as '*Algeriensis variegata*'; somewhere in the mid-1920s it was grown at the Villa Marengo, made its way into Europe, probably as 'Souvenir de Marengo' a name which gave way to 'Gloire de Marengo' under which it circulated modestly prior to World War 2. After the war when house plants increased in popularity 'Gloire de Marengo' was seen as an ideal pot plant. Easily propagated, quick growing and colourful, particularly in its younger stages, it is propagated by the million and must be known in public buildings everywhere that ivy is grown. In view of Jackman's earlier and very fair description of it as 'Gloire de Marengo' this would seem to be the proper and most appropriate name.

It is a fast growing, decorative ivy, ideally suited to a high garden or house wall. In Britain it will survive very severe winters but with much loss of leaf and a resulting poor appearance. The plant has been about for many years but one does not see old specimens in northern Europe. In California and the more favoured areas of America it is sometimes used as ground cover beside freeways and in places where grass maintenance is difficult or expensive. Its prime use in Europe is indoors as a pot plant or a trained pyramid.

Habit	Vining.
Stems	Wine-red when young. Internodes 4–5 cm.
Petioles	Wine-red, smooth.
Leaves	Unlobed, occasional vestigial signs of tri-lobing, leaf shape ovate, apex acute, 9–11 cm by 9–11 cm broad. Light green with broken or large areas of silvery grey-green. Some yellow-white variegation usually at the edges and far more pronounced in young shoots and plants. Leaves often slightly cupped, veins not very prominent.

'MARGINO-MACULATA'

The name of this mottled mutant of 'Gloire de Marengo' was coined by Lawrence & Schulze in 1942; it was given varietal status and a Latin description. This was before the clarification of the use of the category 'varietas' for botanical variations of wild origin rather than horticultural selections. However, a further paper by Lawrence (1956) made amends by listing the plant correctly as a clone. Plants of 'Gloire de Marengo' will occasionally mutate to produce this clone which in turn will often produce shoots identical to 'Gloire de Marengo'. In recent years the plant has become known in the trade as 'Marmorata' and unfortunately, since several ivies in the past have been given this name, it is confusing as well as invalid.

Extensively grown by the pot-plant trade and easily propagated, its rapid growth and bright colouring make it a useful plant for large pyramids and general decorative work. It grows well and fast outdoors in good summers and survives mild winters in Britain but can be badly hit by cold winds or temperatures below $-4°$C ($25°$F). Pierot (1974) quotes it as grown outdoors on the West Coast of the USA but records that she would not grow it farther north than South Connecticut.

Habit   Vining.
Stems   Wine-red when young. Internodes 4–5 cm.
Petioles   Wine-red and smooth.
Leaves   Ovate, unlobed with vestigial signs of tri-lobing, apex
           acute, 9–11 cm by 9–11 cm. Base colour light green ex-
           tensively mottled yellow-white. Occasional leaves parti-
           coloured. Veins not prominent.

'RAVENSHOLST'

Plants of a large-leaved *canariensis* type ivy began to circulate in Britain under this name about 1972 but the origin of the clone remains a mystery. I assume it to be of Dutch or German origin but can find no references to it. Very vigorous with larger leaves than *canariensis* it makes lush and effective ground cover but would appear to be suitable for mild climates only. In most of Britain it suffers badly in sharp winters unless in a sheltered spot. Its USA hardiness is probably limited to Zone 6.

Habit   Vining and vigorous.
Stems   Wine-red, smooth. Internodes 5–7 cm.
Petioles   Wine-red except in deep shade, smooth.
Leaves   Tri-lobed 10–13 cm by 8–14 cm. Centre lobe acute and
           broad. Laterals acute but little more than protrusions.
           Sinuses very shallow, many leaves unlobed and elliptical.
           Leaf base truncate. Dark glossy green, veins lighter.

47

This is most likely the plant described by the nurseryman William Paul (1867) as '*Hedera canariensis aurea-maculata*. Leaves sometimes green but usually green finely clouded with gold, large, growth free and rapid'. Paul's description was accepted and published by the German botanist Karl Koch in 1870. Unfortunately, *Hedera canariensis* and its varieties became confused with the Irish Ivy (*H. helix* 'Hibernica') and Paul's name was used to describe forms of 'Hibernica'. It is as well therefore that Lawrence & Schulze (1942), although not recognising Paul's name, whose validity might be in some doubt, took it upon themselves to describe this ivy and to select for it a distinctive name.

It is a vigorous grower, free and rapid, as Paul stated, useful for walls or fences and very suitable as robust ground cover for fairly sheltered areas. Like the other *canariensis* clones its USA limit is probably Zone 6. The plant has circulated in Britain under the synonyms 'Gold Leaf' and 'Golden Leaf'.

Habit	Vining and vigorous.
Stems	Wine-red. Glabrous with few hairs. Internodes 5–7 cm.
Petioles	Wine-red, almost hairless. Petiole colour sometimes extending along veins on underside of leaves for 1–4 cm.
Leaves	Deltoid, unlobed, 8–14 cm by 10–19 cm. Occasional vestigial indications of tri-lobing. Margin entire and slightly waved, some undulation of leaf surface with apex often down-pointing. Lustrous dark green with a very slight yellow to light green variegation or 'splash' at the leaf centre. Veins light green, not prominent. Spot of red colouring at petiole/leaf-blade junction particularly in older leaves.

Hedera colchica

The Persian or Colchic Ivy is native to the region south of the Caspian and westward through the Caucasus to Asiatic Turkey. The first accurate description is that of Caspar Koch the German botanist and father of Karl Koch, who named it in 1859 *colchica* from its habitat of ancient Colchis. The plant had reached Britain before this, certainly by 1851, and become generally known as *H.*

roegneriana having been found, according to Seeman (1864) by Mr Roegner, 'Formerly Curator of the Botanic Gardens of Odessa'. Although unpublished, this name was widely used and is still occasionally seen today. Hibberd (1872) for no very good reason described the plant as *H. coriacea*, giving *colchica*, *Roegneriana* and *cordifolia* as synonyms; *caucasica* is another invalid name that has been used.

It is a useful ivy but one whose garden utility is overshadowed by that of its large-leaved, more vigorous clone 'Dentata'. Slower growing and less easy to propagate than 'Dentata' it is the true Bullock's Heart ivy; Elephant's Ears is a name more appropriate to 'Dentata'. The scale-like hairs and the resinous odour of the crushed leaves are typical of the species.

The true *colchica* is seldom seen outside botanic gardens but is a suitable variety if a hardy, dark-green, slow-growing ivy is required for a specific situation. The plant called 'My Heart' by Suzanne Pierot in *The Ivy Book* would appear to be identical to *colchica*. In the following description the dimensions given are those seen in Britain; in its native habitat leaves would be much larger.

Habit	Vining.
Stems	Green. Internodes 4–6 cm. Hairs scale-like, 15–20 rays.
Petioles	Green.
Leaves	Ovate, generally unlobed, 6–12 cm by 6–8 cm, margins entire, apices acute, leaf base cordate. Veins thick but recessed in the upper surface of the blade and correspondingly extruded on the under surface. Dark green.

'DENDROIDES'

This ivy, now seen only in botanic gardens or plantsmen's collections has received little mention over the years. The only references I have found are those of Hibberd (1872) and Tobler (1912). It has not, to my knowledge, appeared in any nurseryman's catalogue. Hibberd's description which follows is the only one we have.

DENDROIDES – *Tree-like thick leaved ivy* (syn. *Roegneriana arborea*). – An extraordinary plant, and the most tree-like of all the ivies. It branches freely, forming stout wood. The leaves differ but little from those of the climbing form, but are less inclined to produce lobes, and are usually somewhat narrower and more smooth and glossy. This may be mistaken for a rhododendron when the leaves become narrowed by pot-culture.

Tobler made no mention of it in his text, merely including the name in his list of varieties.

I think Hibberd was mistaken in bracketing it with *Roegneriana arborea*, the tree-form of what we know as *H. colchica*. The plant that has come down to us as 'Dendroides' is not a tree-form; it will climb or sprawl along the ground, throwing out massive shoots which will grow 90 cm (3 ft) in one season and has a stem diameter of $1-1.5$ cm ($\frac{1}{2}-\frac{3}{4}$ in). The scale-hairs and leaves are typical of *colchica* but there appear to be two forms in existence, one whose glossy leaves are those of *colchica* and another having lighter green, slightly toothed leaves which, although smaller, are like those of *colchica* 'Dentata'. Both forms, although woody, do not resemble the usual Tree Ivies that result from rooting cuttings of adult *colchica* stems.

The plant's origin is a mystery but I suspect it may be linked to references to *amurensis* and *acuta* that circulated towards the end of the last century. It is possible that the name 'Amurensis' which has persisted, refers to the Amur River region of Manchukuo. *The Flora of the USSR*, compiled by the USSR'S Botanic Institute, makes no mention of 'Amurensis' or 'Dendroides' but with *Hedera rhombea* indigenous to nearby Japan it would seem feasible that there are species in the Amur region and that 'Dendroides' may have come from that area in the late nineteenth century when trade and travel were expanding.

Habit	Vining or sprawling.
Stems	Brown-purple, thick, becoming woody. Internodes 6–8 cm.
Petioles	Green, short.
Leaves	Ovate, 5–8 cm by 6–8 cm. Generally unlobed. Leaf apex acute, base cordate. Veins depressed giving the leaf blade a puckered appearance. Glossy dark green. Another form has lightly toothed, matt, light-green leaves.

The *most effective* of all ivies, enormous glossy green drooping leaves *10" long, 8" across*. In a developed plant it ascends to a great height and where an evergreen climber is required *nothing can equal it* as it will thrive on a North or East wall and quickly make a show.

This description is taken from a 1910 catalogue of V. N. Gauntlett & Co Ltd, then of Chiddingfold, Surrey, a celebrated firm of nurserymen whose plant list was prefaced by two pages of closely printed names of patrons, some 650 in all, commencing with Prince Henry of Battenberg and descending in order of nobility to Rev. The Hon A. R. Parker. This may seem curiously sycophantic today, but it must be remembered that those were the people who had the means and the will to buy plants; certainly, Gauntlett built up a vast trade. The villagers of Chiddingfold became accustomed to processions of carts to and from the nurseries, for Gauntlett imported much of what he sold. It is probable that the plants making the impressive ivy wall at Polesden Lacey, Surrey, once the home of the Hon. Mrs Roland Greville and a resort of King Edward VII and Edwardian society and now a National Trust property, came from Gauntletts. All that remains of the firm is a most impressive catalogue, found in many horticultural libraries and descriptions, such as that of *Hedera colchica* 'Dentata', that can hardly be bettered.

Hedera colchica is native to the Caucasus, the Balkans and Asia Minor and our knowledge of the discovery of 'Dentata', the much better plant, is scanty. An early record is that in the 1868 catalogue of the German nursery firm of Haage & Schmidt as,

Hedera dentata. A new variety with very large leaves. Found in the Caucasus by the traveller Ruprecht. As hardy as the common ivy. The leaves are as large as those of Hedera algeriensis only these are leathery and of a dark green, with their edges toothed, this distinguishes it from all other kinds.

The 'traveller Ruprecht' was presumably Franz Joseph Ruprecht (1814–1870) the German botanist. Such a useful plant rapidly became known and as 'Hedera dentata' appears in British and Continental catalogues from 1869 onwards, usually with very brief descriptions which invariably praise its large rich green leaves and vigorous growth. In 1889 it received a First Class Certificate in the Royal Horticultural Society's ivy trial and 'The Garden' in 1893 recorded that it was unaffected by the great frost. As a variety of *colchica* this is what one would expect. Hibberd reporting in the RHS Journal of 1890 on the ivies cultivated in the RHS Chiswick Gardens, described it as '*Hedera colchica* "Dentata"', a large ovate form of colchica characterised by a few sharp marginal spines'. Nicholson in the *Illustrated Dictionary of Gardening* (1885) described the plant, with a very good illustration, as '*Hedera helix dentata*', but after Hibberd's description of 1890 horticultural writers and gradually nurserymen listed the plant as '*H. colchica* "Dentata"'.

One can add to Gauntlett's encomiums that the plant makes excellent ground cover for large areas; indeed, in parts of Britain it has naturalised itself. Completely hardy in Britain and most of Europe one would expect it to be at home as far north as Zone 5 in USA.

Habit	Vining, vigorous.
Stems	Purple-brown. Internodes 6–10 cm.
Petioles	Green-purple.
Leaves	Large, mature leaves generally 15–20 cm by 15–17 cm. Leaves to 22 cm long not unusual. Unlobed, ovate, the auriculate leaf base gives an irregularly heart-shaped leaf. Leaf margin carries widely spaced fine teeth. On climbing plants the leaves hang down, the older leaves curling inwards at the edges. Colour rich pea-green, veins light green, not unduly prominent.

'DENTATA VARIEGATA'

This is not only the most spectacular of all the hardy ivies but is probably the most showy evergreen climber available to gardeners. Many variegated ivies are less able to withstand frost and cold winds than their green counterparts, but the variegated form of *colchica* 'Dentata' whose geographical range is south-eastern Europe, Asia Minor, and the Caucasus to northern Iran, has shown no sign of being less hardy than the green plant. The large leaves hang in the same manner as the Elephant's Ears of 'Dentata' but are generously splashed with cream-yellow. As a wall plant it is superb, particularly on red-brick walls or as a backcloth for red-berried deciduous shrubs. It is admirable for ground cover since, unlike some ivies, it retains its variegation when on the ground. Vigorous, and making good cover it is increasingly used for this purpose in architectural schemes where a large-scale plant is needed.

The plant made its appearance as '*Hedera dentata variegata*' on 9 July 1907 when it was exhibited before the Floral Committee of the Royal Horticultural Society by L. R. Russell Ltd, then of Richmond, Surrey. The committee were unanimous in giving it an Award of Merit. Its discovery is an example of the keen plantsman's eye of the nurseryman ever alert for some new variation. Mr Russell had seen the plant in a private garden near his Richmond nursery. Realising its novelty and garden possibilities he asked for a few cuttings and propagated it intensively to meet the demand he foresaw. Following its debut at the RHS Show the firm listed it in their catalogue for 1908 in the following terms:

> *Hedera* dentata variegata: (New). For this exceedingly handsome plant I received an AWARD OF MERIT at the Royal Horticultural Show, 9 July 1907. In this variety is added to the grand glossy foliage of the type a broad marginal band of creamy yellow variegation in the young growth, changing to yellowish white as the leaves mature, the plant is of the same robust habit as the parent and is altogether the finest and most striking ivy in commerce, thoroughly hardy, constant in colouring and the foliage does not scorch in the hottest sun (3/6 to 10/6).

In 1908 10/6 (ten shillings and sixpence) would have equalled at least twenty pounds sterling today. The gardening public, the owners of large estates and the numerous middle-class houses with large gardens, rushed to buy. For Russells it must have been for a brief period, as it were, a licence to mint sovereigns: the owner of the garden where the original plant grew approached Mr Russell doubtless hoping for some share in the proceeds. Mr Russell's reply is not recorded and neither is any form of payment; it is likely and perfectly reasonable that he argued that it was he who saw the plant's potential and could justly claim the rewards. The plant has spread far and wide and gardeners wherever ivies will grow are deeply indebted to Mr Russell.

53

I have used the name 'Dentata Variegata' and not the 'dentato-variegata' of Lawrence & Schulze (1942). In this I have followed Bean (1973). Russell's description of 'Dentata variegata', although more eulogistic than scientific, at least did a service to botany in establishing the name, and as this was followed by descriptions in numerous catalogues it came into general use. It is probable that Lawrence & Schulze did not have access to this when they published their paper in 1942 saying that 'No record has been found in the literature of its ever having been formally described'. Since it is purely a variegated form of the recognised *colchica* 'Dentata' I am satisfied that the description in Russell's catalogue can stand and has priority.

Habit   Vining and vigorous.
Stems   Green-brown. Internodes 5–8 cm. Younger portions bearing the indumentation of stellate hairs that characterise *colchica*.
Petioles   Light green to purple-brown on exposed leaves.
Leaves   Ovate, unlobed, 15–20 cm by 10–12 cm. Margins entire with a few scattered, very small, forward-pointing teeth. Leaf margins tend to fold under. Basic colour light green broken by patches of grey-green and with an irregular leaf-margin of deep cream-yellow. Parti-yellow or complete yellow leaves occasionally arise. Texture leathery with a matt surface. When bruised the leaves have the spicy resinous smell associated with *colchica* varieties.

'SULPHUR HEART'

The Colchic ivies are dramatic large-scale evergreen climbers. This clone with its interesting variegation is a useful addition to the few clones available of this species. The plant was in cultivation in Britain before World War 2 as *H. colchica dentata aurea-striata*, but this name was never published. In Boskoop, Holland the plant became known as 'Sulphur Heart' and under this name Nannenga-Bremekamp (1970) described it. In September 1970 Mr Roy Lancaster described it in 'Gardener's Chronicle' as *H. colchica* 'Paddy's Pride' based on a plant growing in Ampfield, Hampshire. Upon further examination he decided this was the same clone as that already published as 'Sulphur Heart'. A fine plant for walls, fences, low balustrades or ground cover, it is sometimes listed in catalogues as 'Gold Leaf' or 'Paddy's Pride'. As is the case with all *colchica* clones a crushed leaf gives off a somewhat resinous fragrance.

Habit   Vining, vigorous.
Stems   Light green to brown with age. Internodes 4–6 cm.
Petioles Light green to purple-brown.
Leaves   Unlobed, large, 10–13 cm by 9–12 cm, cordate. Margin entire save for a few scattered fine teeth. Colour light green with central irregular splashes of yellow or lighter green. Veins slightly lighter green except where they traverse the variegated patch, where they are yellow.

Hedera helix

Native of Europe north to southern Scandinavia and east to western Russia, extending in the south to the rainier parts of Anatolia and the Caucasus, this ivy is found almost everywhere in Britain and the climate there is particularly suited to it. *Hedera helix* was named by Linnaeus (*Species Plantarum*, 1753) taking the old Latin and Greek names. The species was described in some detail in Seeman's revision of the *Hederaceae* (1864) and by Tobler (1912). The most variable of all Hederas, most cultivated clones are of this species. One can find different leaf forms in a walk along almost any English country lane; because of this variation it is not surprising that English Ivy sent to people living abroad often differs widely, each recipient assuming they have the typical form of the plant.

The type described below is the fairly typical common ivy and indeed compares with the very good plate and description of Sowerby (1804). Despite the existence of many attractively leafed clones, large numbers of the common ivy are sold for landscape purposes where substantial areas of absolute hardy ground cover are needed. *H. helix* is unharmed by temperatures down to $-15°$C ($5°$F). Some East European clones, notably 'Baltica', are said to withstand lower temperatures. As cover for buildings, *helix* is an excellent choice, particularly for rural situations. The ivy covering that attractive English pub will more than likely be *helix* or possibly its variant 'Hibernica'. The more decorative clones, e.g. 'Pedata',

55

or 'Deltoidea' are better suited to what might be termed more sophisticated situations.

Habit   Vining.
Stems   Purple-green. Internodes 4–6 cm.
Petioles   Purple-green.
Leaves   Three to five lobed, 4–6 cm by 6–8 cm, the two basal lobes reduced in size to give the typical ivy leaf shape. Lobes wedge-shaped, sinuses shallow, apices bluntly acute. Dark green, veins light green to white.

'ADAM'

The source of the name is not known but it would be natural to link the plant with 'Eva', a clone to which it indeed bears some resemblance. The main differences are the fairly pronounced cuneate leaf base of the young leaves as opposed to the truncate or slightly cordate bases of similar leaves of 'Eva'. There is, too, a colour difference in variegation, 'Adam' tending to be white-cream whereas 'Eva' is more cream-yellow.

The only published record appears to be that of Bean (1973). Available commercially in Britain since about 1968 it is not recorded on the Continent although the plant has certainly been exported to Britain, usually as 'Eva' or without a name. It is not mentioned in American literature. The fairly white variegation makes it an excellent pot plant and it seems hardy outside.

Habit   Self-branching.
Stems   Green-purple. Internodes 1–2 cm.
Petioles   Green-purple.
Leaves   Tri-lobed, 3–4 cm by 3–4 cm. Lobes forward pointing particularly in young leaves. A diagnostic point is the slight sideways 'lean' of the acuminate centre lobe, lateral lobes acute. Leaf base in young leaves cuneate, less so in older leaves. Leaf centre light green greying with maturity. White-cream variegation irregular and mostly at leaf edge.

'ALT HEIDELBERG'

This cultivar was selected in 1972 by Brother Heieck of Neuburg Monastery near Heidelberg. He described the leaves as being similar to those of *Quercus × schochiana* which indicates the extent to which this plant differs from the usual conception of an ivy. Short jointed and compact and unusual in that the petioles are virtually non-existent, its leaves resemble small oak leaves. The overall effect is of a useful pot plant for room decoration, certain to arouse comment and of great interest to anyone making an ivy collection. The raiser states it to be a mutation obtained from both 'Procumbens' and 'Chicago Minima'; 'Procumbens' is a name quoted by Jenny (1964) and this is the only reference I can find to 'Procumbens' which is not surprising, for since all ivies are procumbent, 'Procumbens' is not a suitable name to give a variety. It is most likely that 'Alt Heidelberg' was a mutation of a form of 'Pittsburgh', termed 'Chicago' or 'Chicago Minima'. Whatever its origin it is a first rate and most interesting ivy. The proposed name was 'Heidelberg' but this was amended to 'Alt Heidelberg' (Old Heidelberg) to avoid confusion with *Hedera* 'Heidelbergensis' grown at the beginning of the century at the Botanic Gardens, Kew and at that time called the 'Heidelberg Ivy', a large leaved form of *H. colchica* which is no longer grown.

Habit	Self-branching and very short jointed, slow growing.
Stems	Red-brown, slender. Internodes 0.3–1 cm.
Petioles	Virtually non-existent, leaves accordingly are disposed regularly around the stem rather than on one plane as is usual by virtue of twisting petioles.
Leaves	Diamond shaped with bluntly rounded apex and cuneate base. 2–3 cm by 1–1.5 cm wide. Entire, or with vestigial lateral lobes. The cuneate base runs out into a short, flat, fluted stalk so that the leaf is sessile. Colour deep green, younger leaves shiny, older ones dull. Veins on older leaves light green.

'ANGULARIS'

First described by Hibberd (1872), Charles Turner of Slough, to whom Hibberd had sold his collection, was the only nurseryman to list this plant until L. R. Russell Ltd, of Richmond, Surrey, listed it as a 'Pale green' variety; other nurserymen followed and it was catalogued occasionally until the 1930s. It may be seen in many old gardens but has not been commercially grown for some while.

The variety was grown in the Royal Horticultural Society's gardens at Chiswick in 1890, and Hibberd reporting on the ivies said 'Angularis is a Jersey ivy with large leaves angular in form and of a light green colour'. This differs from his earlier, and I think, more accurate description, 'Leaves of medium size, bright green, and glossy, having no peculiarity of conformation sufficiently striking to arrest the attention of a casual observer ... boundaries of the side lobes approximate to straight lines.' There is little to add to this: its bright-green leafage makes it rather more interesting than common *H. helix* when an ordinary green climbing ivy is required. It is plentiful on the Channel Islands.

Habit   Vining.
Stems   Green, faintly tinged purple. Internodes 3–4.5 cm.
Petioles   Green tinged purple.
Leaves   Three lobed, 4–5 cm by 5–7 cm. Centre lobe cuspid, occasionally wedge-shaped, lateral lobes wedge-shaped, sinuses shallow. Sides of lateral lobes often straight. Vestigial basal lobes occasionally produce a 'stepped' leaf outline. Leaf base slightly auriculate. Colour fresh bright green. Veins lighter but not noticeably so.

'ANGULARIS AUREA'

Hibberd (1872) described with accuracy 'Angularis', the bright green, glossy leaved ivy that is generally conceded as being a Channel Islands form. Strangely, however, when reviewing the Royal Horticultural Society's Trial of Ivies held at Chiswick (RHS Journal, 1890), he described the golden variegated form of it, entered in the Trial as 'Angularis Aurea', as 'Chrysophylla'; thereafter there was some confusion between the two names. Various nurserymen, however, continued to list both, in particular William Clibran & Son of Altrincham, Cheshire. The description of 'Angularis Aurea' in their 1894 catalogue together with those of the firm of L. R. Russell Ltd in their catalogues from 1908 to 1932 identify it as the plant grown today and listed by present-day nurserymen. 'Chrysophylla' was the earliest, and therefore the correct, name for a similar clone circulating in the 1890s and since as 'Spectabilis

Aurea'. The variegated form of 'Angularis' would be easily confused with it. (See 'Chrysophylla' below, p. 69.)

The name is sometimes listed as 'Angularia Aurea' but I have followed the RHS Dictionary (1951) which lists it as 'Angularis Aurea', preserving more distinctly its link with 'Angularis'.

Habit	Vining.
Stems	Green, faintly tinged purple. Internodes 1.5–2.5 cm.
Petioles	Green.
Leaves	Three lobed, 4–5 cm by 5–6 cm. Centre lobe cuspid, occasionally wedge-shaped, sinuses shallow. Sides of lateral lobes often straight. Vestigial basal lobes produce a 'stepped' leaf outline, leaf base slightly auriculate. Bright green, some leaves suffused with interveinal deep yellow, surface glossy.

'ANNA MARIE'

A popular ivy, mass produced for the pot-plant trade. Originating from Denmark it was probably a mutation from 'Harald' which it resembles in colour but differs from in its larger, rounded lobed leaves. Self-branching but making sufficient trails to be suitable for hanging baskets as well as pots and troughs. It may be planted outside in sheltered spots for low walls but in Britain suffers in hard winters. The clone 'Anne Borch' is said to be similar but with smaller leaves.

Habit	Self-branching with short trails.
Stems	Green-light purple. Internodes 2–3 cm.
Petioles	Green.
Leaves	Five lobed, 3–4.5 cm by 5–6 cm. Sinuses so shallow as to render the lobing indistinct. Apices obtuse to round. Basic colour medium green with grey-green areas. Clear cream variegation mostly at the leaf edge. Veins light green, not prominent.

'ARDINGLY'

This attractive short-jointed variegated ivy was found by Mrs Hazel Key in a garden in Ardingly, Sussex. The leaf shape and colour suggest that it may be a mutation from 'Glacier'. Very close growing, the pink-purple stems appear like a net-work among the white-grey leaves. A good pot plant or suited in Britain for sheltered outdoor situations where on the flat it will make an attractive hummock or clad a low wall.

Habit   Self-branching.
Stems   Pink-purple. Internodes 1–2 cm.
Petioles Pink-purple.
Leaves   Irregularly three lobed, 1.5–2 cm by 2–3 cm. One lobe often larger than the other, apex bluntly acute. Irregularly rimmed cream, basic colour mid-green with broken areas of grey-green.

'ATROPURPUREA'

The so-called 'Purple Ivy' this is sometimes listed by nurserymen under the erroneous names of 'Purpurea' or 'Nigra'. It is a clone whose origin is reasonably certain as the following extract, a contribution by W. Brockbank to the horticultural periodical 'The Garden' of 24 January 1885 shows:

> The late Thomas Williams of Ormskirk found a wild variety with deep purple leaves which deepened in colour almost to black and he called it Hedera purpurescens. Mr Williams sold his stock of this ivy, I believe, to Messrs Backhouse of York and they brought it out as a novelty a few years back under the name of Hedera atropurpurea.

The plant had been mentioned in 'The Garden' of 1884 as a suitable variety 'To contrast with the large golden ivy' and from this time on, various catalogues listed it either as *purpurea* or *atropurpurea*. Hibberd did not mention the plant; his *purpurea* (1872) was a variety of *Hedera colchica* but the plant he described as *nigra* may well have been 'Atropurpurea' because when reporting in the Royal Horticultural Society's Journal of 1889/90 on the trial of ivies held at Chiswick, he suggested that, *nigra* and *atropurpure* are synonymous'. The leaves of the plant are not, in summer, the 'deep purple' suggested by the writer in 'The Garden' but certainly turn that shade in winter.

Habit	Vining.
Stems	Purple. Internodes 1.5–3 cm.
Petioles	Purple.
Leaves	Five lobed, 4–6 cm by 5–7 cm. Basal-lobes vestigial, sinuses shallow, centre lobe prolonged to acuminate, laterals bluntly acute. Leaf texture thin. Dull dark green in summer colouring to deep purple in winter, depth of colour increases with exposure to cold and in open situation.

'BIG DEAL'

This is one of those ivies with leaves totally unlike an ivy – wherein lies much of its fascination. Raised and introduced from America in the early 1970s and called the Geranium Ivy on account of the similarity of its rounded puckered leaves to those of the greenhouse geranium. Essentially a house plant, 'Big Deal' makes an interesting pot or trough plant; the stems are a little too stiff to recommend it for hanging baskets.

Habit	Self-branching with short trails.
Stems	Red-purple, noticeably smooth and slightly zig-zag, i.e. diverging in direction from node to node. Internodes 3–6 cm.
Petioles	Red-purple-green.
Leaves	Unlobed, 4–6 cm by 3–6 cm, sufficiently auriculate to hide the petiole junction. Colour medium green. Veins radiating from the petiole, raised and thread-like. Leaf margins slightly puckered giving a slight cupped effect to the leaf.

'BOSKOOP'

This mutation from 'Green Ripple', found by J. A. Boer of Boskoop was introduced by him in 1961 and awarded a Silver Medal at the Flora Nova in Boskoop in the same year. It was described and figured by Harry van de Laar in 1965 and by Dr Nannenga-Bremekamp in 1970. An identical mutation was selected at the Epheu Stauss nursery near Stuttgart in the early 1970s from 'Maple Queen'. This is interesting when one recalls that 'Green Ripple' was a mutation selected by Hahn in America from 'Maple Queen' as long ago as 1939. Tighter and less vining than 'Green Ripple' its curled leaves and rich green make 'Boskoop' a most useful pot plant.

Habit   Self-branching.
Stems   Green-purple. Internodes 2–3.5 cm.
Petioles Green-purple.
Leaves   Five lobed, 5–8 cm by 4–7 cm. Lobes wedge-shaped, centre lobe longer than laterals and acuminate. Laterals forward pointing and acute, leaf base cuneate, basal lobes reduced. All lobes down-pointing giving a 'claw' look to the leaf. Sinuses narrow with leaf margin raised at the cleft giving a frilled appearance. Bright green, veins raised but similar in colour.

'BROKAMP'

Examination of this and the clone 'Gavotte' gives the impression that both are the same, and indeed differences are hard to detect. They were, however, selected from different clones and separately described and are treated so here.

'Brokamp' was selected from what has been known in the plant trade in both America and Europe as 'Sagittifolia'. The selection was made at the Brokamp Nursery, Ramsdorf, Westfalen, Germany and described by O. Koch in 'Gartenwelt' in 1959 and by Jenny (1964). Herr Brokamp named it '*H. helix* salicifolia typ. Brokamp'; this was shortened to 'Brokamp' but the plant is still often called 'salicifolia'. In trying to detect differences between this and 'Gavotte' one can discern a tendency in it to develop a rounded lobe on one side of the predominantly lanceolate leaves and the appearance of a few sagittate leaves. Because of this it is important to maintain the stock by propagating only from shoots with willow-like leaves. Apart from this and indeed under any name the willow-like leaves of this ivy make it an interesting and useful plant. It is reasonably hardy in Britain and probably Zone 7 in America. Throwing long trails it is useful for hanging baskets and the plant is vigorous enough to provide ground cover for small areas.

Habit   Self-branching but with long trails.
Stems   Green-purple. Internodes 1.5–3 cm.
Petioles Green. 0.5–2 cm.

Leaves	Mostly entire and lanceolate, 5 cm long by 1–1.5 cm wide, acuminate. Occasional leaves with an asymmetrical lateral lobe also some sagittate leaves. Central vein prominent, lateral veins running almost parallel. Medium green to a much lighter green in summer.

'BRUDER INGOBERT'

This mutation from 'Glacier' was selected by Brother Ingobert Heieck in 1962 at the Neuburg Abbey Nursery, Heidelberg. Its variable leaf shapes and its leaf colour which includes deep green and cream-white make it a more interesting plant than its parent. Primarily useful as a house plant or for hanging baskets, it is suitable also for low walls.

Habit	Vining and moderately branching.
Stems	Purple-red. Internodes 1.5–3 cm.
Petioles	Purple-red. In general shorter than those of 'Glacier'.
Leaves	Indistinctly three to five lobed. Many leaves irregularly shaped and indented. 2–3.5 cm by 3–5 cm. Lobes rounded, sinuses shallow or non-existent. Leaf blade undulating, leaf base deeply cordate. Colour basically grey-green with irregular dark-green patches. Leaves often show a dark-green rim area and an inner rim of cream-white, leaf centre being grey-green. Veins light green, not prominent.

'BUTTERCUP'

One of the most useful and decorative of garden ivies, this can be used in combination with other plants to give some lovely effects while remaining a superb ivy in its own right. 'Buttercup' is a climbing ivy and not to be recommended for ground cover where it will lose its unique golden colouring.

I cannot trace any plant with similar characteristics in the early literature, although the nursery firm of T. Smith of Newry, Ireland, listed in 1925, 'Buttercup, small brilliant golden leaved', while the firm of L. R. Russell Ltd, who specialised in ivies between 1900 and 1939, listed various golden-leaved varieties, some of whose descriptions would fit 'Buttercup'. Russells, like all British

63

nurseries, were badly hit by the restrictions of World War 2 which limited the growing of ornamentals, and they lost many interesting varieties. Some of these may have survived the war years in America, a theory suggested by the comments of Lawrence & Schulze (1942) who, describing an ivy 'Russell Gold', stated that it was donated by C. Mc. K. Lewis of Sloatsburg, New York who had obtained the material from L. R. Russell Ltd, in 1934. This plant which has returned to Britain from the States does not appear to be as good a grower as 'Buttercup' which according to Pierot (1974) is hardy south of New York.

Habit	Vining. Colouring better in a good light situation.
Stems	Green in the shade to green-yellow in the sun. Internodes 1–2.5 cm.
Petioles	Green.
Leaves	Five lobed, 5–7 cm by 6–8 cm. Apices acute, sinuses shallow, centre lobe slightly prolonged. Colour light green in shade, in sun some leaves green-yellow, others complete yellow.

'CAENWOODIANA AUREA'

For many years the green Bird's Foot Ivy, now called 'Pedata', was known as *caenwoodiana*. In 1905 a reference to a yellow-leaved form was listed without description, in Robert Veitch's catalogue. A descriptive note appeared in the 1908 catalogue of L. R. Russell Ltd, then of Richmond, Surrey: 'Caenwoodiana aurea – foliage heavily blotched yellow.' The clone was listed thereafter in various catalogues, the last being Hillier's of Winchester, Hampshire, in 1924. Their catalogue of 1928, while listing the usual green 'Caenwoodiana', said 'The golden form is not sufficiently constant' and the last reference is in the Royal Horticultural Society's Journal for 1930 where it is noted among plants suitable for a north wall. As indicated in the extract from Hillier's catalogue the plant fell out of favour, but such is the tenacity of ivy that it has survived in at least two large gardens in Britain. It is true to say that it is only of interest to those specialising in ivies and building up collections, but it can of course be used for the same garden purposes as 'Pedata'. In habit and growth it is the same, the only difference being in leaf colour. The suffusion of light yellow is seen in spring in the young leaves. In young plants this is rapidly replaced by the normal green colour but in older plants and particularly in a moist, light shade position the colour is retained in some leaves at least. It is essentially a wall ivy.

Habit	Vining.
Stems	Green-purple. Internodes 2–5 cm.
Leaves	Five lobed, the central lobe approximately one-third longer than the laterals and tending to be narrower at the base and broader at the middle, tapering to the tip, 4–5 cm by 5–6 cm. The lobes are back pointing giving the Bird's Foot appearance and accounting for the popular name. The younger leaves gradually take on a yellow coloration as they develop, although subsequent leaves attain the usual grey-green associated with 'Pedata', similarly the veins are light green.

'CALIFORNIA FAN'

An attractive self-branching ivy hailing from America and not as well known in Europe as it should be. The prominent veins and the manner in which they radiate enhance the fan-like shape of the soft green leaves. Excellent as a pot plant, for troughs, etc., produces short trails but too slowly for hanging baskets. Hardy in USA Zone 6, suffers in severe winters in Britain and northern Europe where it is essentially an indoor ivy.

Habit	Self-branching.
Stems	Green-pink. Internodes 1.5–3 cm.
Petioles	Green-pink.
Leaves	Five to seven lobed 3–4 cm by 4–5 cm. Lobes bluntly acute and forward pointing. Leaf base truncate or sometimes attenuated. Light green, veins raised and prominent.

'CALIFORNIA GOLD'

Listed by Graf (1963) as 'A mutant of "Weber Californian" with rather rounded leaves light green marbled with yellow, especially in younger leaves. Stays self-branching and bushy.' Pierot (1974) points to the plant's habit of occasional whole or half-green leaves. Jenny (1964) is the only one to draw attention to the wavy lobes of this clone, the chief difference between it and 'Luzii' and similar yellow variegated clones. The overall effect makes a decorative and useful pot ivy.

Habit   Self-branching and compact.
Stems   Pink-purple. Internodes 1–1.5 cm.
Petioles   Green-purple.
Leaves   Five lobed, 3–5 cm by 4–7 cm. Lobes obtuse to rounded, often irregular. Leaf base cordate, sinuses fairly deep, convoluted at clefts. Basic colour light green marbled yellow-cream. Veins cream, fairly prominent.

'CASCADE'

Registered with the American Ivy Society under 752, this clone originated in south-east Virginia and was introduced by Mr W. L. Swicewood of Rescue, Virginia. Very similar to 'Merion Beauty' it has the same self-branching tendency as good stocks of that, but has more colour in the stem, is more strongly veined and has crimped leaves. Its tendency to throw long, branching trails make it an excellent plant for hanging baskets.

Habit   Self-branching with extending vines.
Stem   Purple-green.
Petioles   Green-purple.
Leaves   Five lobed, basal lobes rather reduced, 2–3 cm by 2–3 cm. Sinuses shallow, ridged at the cleft giving a crisp feel to the leaves. Centre lobe wedge-shaped, laterals more obtuse. Colour mid-green, veins much lighter.

'CAVENDISHII'

First mentioned by Paul (1867), I have been unable to trace the origin of the name but it may be assumed to honour the family name of the Dukes of Devonshire. At this period the Duke's gardener, Joseph Paxton, later Sir Joseph, had distinguished himself as the gardener at Chatsworth and as the architect of the Crystal Palace, and it seems likely that the name was bestowed to attract attention to the variety. Various plants bear the specific *cavendishii* in honour of the celebrated gardens and the equally noted gardener and one can assume that Paul, a leading nurseryman of his day, named the plant which may have already been in circulation. The name does not appear in catalogues or lists published prior to his article in the 'Gardener's Chronicle'. The only other possible link might be with the village of Cavendish in Suffolk, but so far I have found no connection there. In 1870 Paul's list was copied, with acknowledgements, by Karl Koch, the celebrated German botanist, receiving what may be termed botanical blessing and giving the name a validity recognised by Lawrence & Schulze (1942).

It was Hibberd in 1872 who queered the nomenclatural pitch when in his book *The Ivy* he described a plant as 'Marginata minor', listing *cavendishii* as one of its synonyms, his aversion to personal names asserting itself once more. Nicholson (1885) followed Hibberd's lead, but Bean (1914) described the plant as *cavendishii*. Nurserymen, understandably, were confused; some managed to list both 'Cavendishii' and 'Marginata minor'! Regardless of this, the plant, by virtue of its good constitution and good variegation, persisted in gardens.

I suspect that 'Cavendishii', although listed as 'new' in catalogues around 1868, may be the original 'Silver Striped' ivy of Richard Weston (1770) and going back some 1900 years that it may have been the variegated ivy of Pliny (Pliny's *Natural History, 23–79 AD*). My reasoning for this is the fact that the plant never seems to revert, i.e. to throw green leaves. Any plant with a tendency to reversion would, over a long period, without care and cutting out of the green portions, lose its variegation and character. If the 'Silver Striped' of Weston and the variegated of Pliny are still with us, I suggest it must be in the form of a non-reverting kind such as 'Cavendishii'.

For today's gardener it remains an excellent, easy, hardy, variegated climber. In arborescence which it achieves readily, it produces black fruits profusely and in this form can be used as a 'spot' plant. It is not suited to ground cover.

Habit   Vining.
Stems   Light green. Internodes 1–3 cm.
Petioles Green.

Leaves   Three lobed, 5–6 cm by 6–7 cm. Lobes acutely pointed
          and angular in the young leaves, less so with maturity.
          Sinuses shallow, leaf base truncate. Lobes sometimes
          vestigial in older leaves. Leaf centre medium green,
          sometimes with grey-green streaks, occasionally the
          green breaks through to the irregular margin of cream-
          yellow.

'CHESTER'

A clone that has recently (1979) made its appearance in Europe
under the above name. It has potential as a pot plant and although
nothing seems known of its origin or indeed if this is the correct
name, it seems worthwhile to record it here. It makes a fairly compact self-branching plant; the roughly triangular leaves are a soft
lime-green when young with a substantial well-defined dark-green
centre. As the leaf ages the lime-green area changes to cream-white
so that the leaf looks like a miniature 'Gloire de Marengo'. The
plant propagates well and seems likely to be a good commercial
ivy. Nothing is known of its capabilities outdoors.

Habit   Self-branching with short trails.
Stems   Green-purple. Internodes 2–2.5 cm.
Petioles Green-purple.
Leaves   Remotely three lobed, 3–3.5 cm by 4.5–5 cm. The shal-
          low sinuses give a leaf almost triangular in outline.
          Apices acute, leaf base deeply cordate. Ground colour
          lime-green in young leaves with dark-green central
          splash. As leaf ages ground colour turns cream-white,
          central portion darkens.

'CHICAGO'

A clone, indeed several clones, under this name have circulated
in Europe from about 1962 and been catalogued by various nurseries. The published references of Jenny (1964), Van de Laar
(1965) and Nannenga-Bremekamp (1970) all agree in describing
it as a small-leaved clone of 'Pittsburgh'. It is probable that the
original 'Pittsburgh' is now seldom seen, most nurseries, cons-
ciously or unconsciously having selected the smaller-leaved

material when propagating so that 'Chicago' has supplanted its parent largely through selection. A most useful and widely grown pot plant, it will also make good ground cover, preferably in open situations for it is not reliable for this purpose under trees. Stocks vary considerably but that described below is judged to be typical.

Habit   Self-branching.
Stems   Red-green. Internodes 2–4 cm.
Petioles Pink-green.
Leaves   Three lobed, 3–4 cm by 3–4 cm. Centre lobe only slightly longer than laterals, lobes acute, sinuses shallow. Most leaves show two very slight basal lobes. Leaf base cordate, colour light green.

'CHRYSOPHYLLA'

This ivy is generally referred to in catalogues at the present time as 'Spectabilis Aurea' or sometimes 'Aurea Spectabilis'. No record exists, however, of a published description under these names whereas it is clear that Hibberd (1872) and in his report on the Royal Horticultural Society's Ivy Trial in 1890 was describing the same plant. There is an earlier reference to 'Chrysophylla', namely that in the 1867 catalogue of Robert Veitch & Sons of Exeter, who describe the plant as follows, 'Some of the leaves of H. helix chrysophylla are yellow, others green and others blotched with yellow, it is very rich and distinct.' Hibberd when reporting on the varieties in the RHS Trial wrote,

Chrysophylla is variable and uncertain and needs to be kept to the best possible character by propagating from the best coloured growths obtainable. It is well known as a fast-growing ivy of robust habit; the leaves occasionally richly coloured deep yellow in patches or in a mottled form, justify one of its names of 'Clouded Gold'. Contributed by Mr Turner as 'Spectabilis Aurea' and by Mr Fraser as 'Gold Clouded'. The plant sent by Mr Turner as 'Angularis aurea' is Chrysophylla in one of its many forms differing but little from the type.

In fairness to 'Mr Turner' (this was Charles Turner (1818–85) the celebrated Slough nurseryman who 'promoted' the then unknown Cox's Orange Pippin apple) it should be said that the ivy generally known in the trade as 'Spectabilis Aurea' had been offered as such in various catalogues since about 1870. The last comment of Hibberd's description shows that confusion between this clone and 'Angularis Aurea' is by no means new. Colouring and habit are indeed similar but the leaves of 'Angularis Aurea' tend to be thinner, the green parts a lighter green and the primary veins less noticeable. As the leaves age they take on an angled appearance with typically an elliptic centre lobe terminating in a slightly drawn out apex. The leaves of 'Chrysophylla' on the other hand are basically three lobed with the lobes wedge-shaped, the leaf thicker in texture and of a deeper green.

Differentiating between the two clones is a slightly academic exercise; both are excellent for wall cover; 'Chrysophylla' probably shows more colour as the plants mature. 'Angularis Aurea' shows better yellow colour when young and is the more suitable clone for ground cover.

Habit	Vining.
Stems	Green, sometimes tinged purple. Internodes 2.5–4 cm.
Petioles	Green.
Leaves	Three lobed, 4–6 cm by 5–8 cm. Lobes wedge-shaped and almost equal. Leaf base truncate. Medium to deep green, some leaves suffused light yellow. Main veins fairly pronounced. Can be confused with 'Angularis Aurea' whose leaves are thinner, light green, more indented and with a cuspid centre lobe and less prominent veins. Adult leaves of 'Chrysophylla' are spear-shaped, those of 'Angularis Aurea' more pointed.

'COCKLE SHELL'

One of the most interesting ivies in that it is utterly unlike an ivy. In place of the usual three- or five-lobed leaf is an almost round leaf, attractively veined and concave. Essentially a house-plant ivy, 'Cockle Shell' is one of the fascinating number of mutants that have developed in America. Recorded in 1976 'Cockle Shell' is a mutant of 'California' and was found by Paul Taylor of Rosemeade, California. The plant was registered by Mrs Marion Vincent of La Habra, California, with the American Ivy Society as 'Cockle Shell'

(Reg. No. 762). In America reputedly hardy in Zone 7 it has so far proved hardy in Britain and an attractive clone for hanging baskets and indoor cultivation.

Habit   Self-branching.
Stems   Light purple. Internodes 2–2.5 cm.
Petioles   Light purple.
Leaves   3–5 cm long by the same in breadth, often unlobed and appearing almost circular but occasionally showing three to five vestigial lobes, often as little more than marginal protrusions. Leaf margins upturned giving the leaf blade the concavity aptly described by its name. Light green maturing to dark green. Veins light green, prominent, raised, radiating in digital fashion from the petiole junction.

'CONGESTA'

This is the name widely used on the European continent for the small-leaved erect ivy. (For the history of the erect ivies see 'Erecta'.) An allied clone 'Conglomerata', whether growing on a wall, over a rock stone or on the ground is essentially a climber. Occasionally it throws what appear to be erect shoots and it may be that the erect ivies arose from shoots of this kind. Whatever its origin this ivy is of great architectural value as a rock-garden plant and better for the small garden than its larger cousin 'Erecta'. Leaves are smaller and the stems tend to have more colour, the distichous leaf arrangement is tighter. Sometimes misnamed as 'Erecta', 'Minima' or 'Conglomerata Minima'. A specimen in the Kew Herbarium collected by a certain 'M. Young' in 1887 and labelled 'Hedera helix minima, Milford Nursery, Godalming' is certainly 'Congesta'.

Habit   Non-climbing, erect.
Stems   Short jointed, green-purple. Internodes 0.5–1 cm.
Petioles   Light green.
Leaves   Three lobed, 3–4 cm by 2–3 cm. Sinuses shallow, young leaves unlobed. Apex acute, leaf margins lift to give a folded effect, this combined with the two-ranked leaf arrangement gives a very formal plant. Dark green, veins light green.

The origins of many ivy clones are elusive, few more so than this, which is so different in stature and appearance from most ivies that one would have supposed its discovery would excite considerable comment. This did not seem to be the case. The first record is that in the 'Gardener's Chronicle' of 10 June 1871. Reporting the Royal Horticultural Society's meeting of the 7 June, it recorded that 'A new ivy named *Hedera conglomerata* was then alluded to as being an interesting addition to this class of plants on account of its distinct habit'. These comments were picked up by continental writers; *La Belgique Horticole* of 1873 commented, 'It is one of the most curious and distinct varieties of ivy' and in 1875 it was listed by the German firm of Haage & Schmidt. Lawrence (1956) suggests that it arose in Germany in 1870 but gives no reference to the source of this information. The first British catalogue reference is that of B. S. Williams, Upper Holloway, London, where in 1878 it is listed as a variety of *helix* but without description. William Clibran & Son of Altrincham, listed it in 1880 as 'Very distinct with curiously distorted foliage', thereafter it was in wide circulation. References appeared in the horticultural press; 'The Garden' for 12 February 1881 wrote of it as,

> The clustered ivy, Hedera conglomerata. This is a peculiar ivy and quite distinct from its congeners both in foliage and habit. The leaves are very thick and have a curious crimped appearance, while the plant instead of climbing forms a low spreading shrub suitable for the shady parts of rockwork and similar places.

In 1889, following an Award of Merit after trial in the Royal Horticultural Society's gardens at Chiswick, Shirley Hibberd wrote in the Society's Journal

> Hedera conglomerata has the merits of distinctness and though scarcely beautiful is immensely interesting. The growth is in a somewhat geometric plan the branches radiating regularly. The leaves are ovate, curled and frilled and overlap so as to form a dense imbricated mass, the result as may be seen of a peculiar fasciation. The colour is a deep rich green. When trained to a wall its character is destroyed, it should be left perfectly free to spread in its own way on an open border or on a broad shelf

in the rockery. It requires a moist warm climate to ensure full development.

Hibberd did not mention the plant in his monograph of 1872 which would have been printing in 1871 so it is fair to assume that the record of 10 June 1871 was the first public appearance of the clone.

In 'Revue Horticole' – 1890, Carrière described the plant adequately but with a poor illustration. Nicholson's *Dictionary of Gardening* (1885) depicted it as 'A marked slow growing erect variety with small wavy leaves and very short internodes. An excellent subject for rockwork'. The word 'Erect' seems a misnomer and may have bred the confusion seen in subsequent catalogues between this and 'Erecta'; certainly his illustration does not depict an erect variety. Tobler (1912) listed the variety without description, quoting Haage & Schmidt's catalogue of 1875; Bean (1973) describes it as 'A dwarfed, very slow growing form, the leaves small and crowded, much crinkled and undulate. Stems stout, procumbent, slightly flattened when young'. In this he endorses the descriptions of those who in the 1870s first discussed this variety but unhappily for us left no record of where it arose or who brought it to notice. In all events it has retained its identity, does not appear to revert and has not thrown any variegated form. It remains the 'clustered Ivy suitable for rockwork' and can be strongly recommended for this purpose. It is also suitable for low walls, making slow but close cover with its thick wavy leaves.

Habit	Creeping and climbing, very short jointed.
Stems	Short jointed, often slightly flattened, green. Internodes 0.5–1 cm.
Petioles	Light green.
Leaves	Unlobed to obscurely three lobed, 1–3 cm by 2–4 cm. Margins undulate and waved. Arranged in two ranks. Texture, leathery, dark green. Veins raised giving the leaf surface a puckered appearance.

'CORRUGATA'

An unusual ivy which seems to have been sparsely documented. Hibberd (1872) described it as 'A pretty and distinct tree-ivy, which grows freely and soon forms a handsome pot-plant. The

leaves agree very closely with those of crenata, it bears fruit plenti-
fully.' Fortunately for us he supported this rather inadequate description with an illustration that corresponds exactly with plants
seen today and particularly with material at the Royal Botanic
Gardens, Kew. Hibberd's figure appears to be of adult shoots and
it is true to say that the forward-pointing, almost toothed lobing,
and the attenuated leaf base are more evident on older material.
A most interesting wall ivy of which 'Mrs Pollock' would seem to
be the variegated form.

Habit	Vining.
Stems	Green. Internodes 3–5 cm.
Petioles	Green.
Leaves	Five to seven lobes, 5–7 cm by 6–8 cm. Lobes often appear as little more than forward-pointing projections or large teeth at the apex of a leaf whose cuneate base makes it like an inverted triangle with its apex at the petiole/leaf-blade junction. The lobes are short and acuminate with narrow sinuses. Medium to dark green, soft apple green beneath. Veins light green, very thin and radiating closely from the petiole junction.

'CUSPIDATA MAJOR'

This ivy is easily identified from the illustration in Hibberd's *The
Ivy* (1872) and from his description,

> The lobes uniformly three lobed, all the lobes project forward,
> the centre being the largest; they are cuspid in outline and pecu-
> liarly 'cockled' at the bifurcation. The leaf is thick and hard like
> parchment, colour deep, full cheerful green.

Hibberd quoted *Hibernica palmata* as a synonym, and described
it as a Tree Ivy and it may well be that with its pleasing colourful
foliage and good leaf shape it was sold as *Hedera arborea*, a general
name then for Tree Ivies; certainly 'Cuspidata Major' and 'Hibernica Palmata' were rarely catalogued. The only listing I have found
is that of Barr & Son (1895–9).

The plant, undeniably that described by Hibberd, has been
found as a climber on walls at a few stately homes in Britain, doubtless planted around the turn of the century. A pleasant-looking

plant, its fresh green colour and its almost trident-like leaves are its attributes.

Habit   Vining.
Stem   Green. Internodes 3–5 cm.
Petioles   Green–Purple.
Leaves   Three lobed, 6–7 cm by 5–9 cm. Lobes cuspid or acuminate. Forward pointing so that often the tips of the three lobes are parallel. Sinuses narrow, margin convolute at the cleft. Leaf base cuneate to attenuate. Colour fresh bright green. Veins light green, pointing forward in slowly diverging lines from the petiole/leaf-blade junction.

'CUSPIDATA MINOR'

Although not commercially available, this ivy which is present in one or two collections can be recognised from Hibberd's description (1872):

> A pretty small-leaved variety, distinctly cuspid. The young stems are purplish, and the leaf-stalks are bright reddish-purple. The leaves are placed far apart; they are uniformly three-lobed, and the lobes are equal and crenated, the colour a deep rich glossy green with whitish veins.

The plant as seen today has green stems, light purple at the growing tip and deep green, heart-shaped leaves. It is a neat climber, running quickly and making a distinct 'pattern' but not filling in well; not suited for ground cover. The clone 'Tomboy' described by Nannenga-Bremekamp (1970) and marketed in the USA appears to be the same ivy.

Habit   Vining with long trails.
Stems   Green, light purple towards the tip. Internodes 1–3 cm.
Petioles   Short, 0.5–1 cm, green but with a slight red tinge near the stem junction, more noticeable because of the green stem and leaves.
Leaves   Deltoid or heart-shaped, 2–4 cm by 2.5–3 cm, unlobed or vaguely three-lobed. Margin slightly waved. Leaves are regularly spaced giving a precise almost 'Herring bone' structure to the trails. Although the internodes are

close the leaves being small give the plant an open appearance. Colour deep green, veins light green.

'DEALBATA'

This plant was described by Hibberd (1872) as,

> A very distinct and peculiar plant occurring frequently in a wild state in the woods on the Eastern slopes of Snowdonia, where it frequently carpets the ground with a profuse growth of dark-green leafage, dotted with leaves of a pure white. The leaves are usually equally three-lobed small and varying but little in size or form; many of them dark-green, with a faint powdering of white; others wholly blanched and semi-transparent; when grown in a good soil, the growth becomes wholly green, but when grown in a soil consisting chiefly of potsherds, broken stones, and coarse grit, it continues faithful to its sylvan character.

Strangely there is no subsequent reference in literature or catalogues of the day to the plant, it was not even catalogued by Charles Turner the nurseryman to whom Hibberd sold his collection. Possibly Hibberd noted the plant and collected material but failed to retain it; we do not know. Reviewing the genus, Lawrence & Schulze (1942) assumed it to be the same plant as their 'Discolor', and the 'Minor Marmorata' of Paul, although Hibberd had named both 'Discolor' and 'Dealbata' and with different descriptions of each, all of which is rather confusing and unsatisfactory.

The picture clears, however, when we examine another of the early varieties. In 1928, L. R. Russell Ltd, then of Richmond, Surrey, catalogued *H. helix* 'Howardiana' which they described as 'Edge mottled silver, very pretty in the young growth'. Their 1932 catalogue had the same description but the name was changed to 'Howardi' and from catalogues and literature that is the last we hear of 'Howardi'. There the matter might rest but for the fortunate existence at the Royal Botanic Gardens, Kew of an ivy labelled 'Howardi'. Examination of this very old plant and of cuttings rooted from it, and now three years old, show it to have all the characters of Hibberd's 'Dealbata'. What happened? I suggest the plant is a rare variation of the native *Hedera helix*; Hibberd's plant failed to get established but presumably a second finding (by a Mr Howard?) found its way into Russell's catalogue. Possibly the plant

76

was lost during World War 2 or perhaps discarded because of its tendency to revert to the green of its *helix* ancestry. The plant at Kew is about fifty years old and shows variegation only on a few young shoots. 'Dealbata' differs from 'Minor Marmorata' ('Discolor') in that the leaf is consistently three-lobed while that of 'Minor Marmorata' is five-lobed, broad and with more consistent variegation than 'Dealbata'. A neat climber suitable for small areas of wall. Hibberd's comments as to poor soil should be noted.

Habit	Vining.
Stems	Purple-green, thin. Internodes 3–3.5 cm.
Petioles	Purple, slender.
Leaves	Three lobed, triangular to arrow-shaped, apex acute, 3–5 cm by 4–6 cm. Sinuses shallow or non-existent. Dark green irregularly spotted and splashed cream-white, more noticeable in young leaves.

'DELTOIDEA'

Described and figured by S. Hibberd (1872) as 'The blunt triangular ivy' and noted by him as, 'A dull unattractive plant, strikingly interesting to an amateur of ivies.' Known generally as the Shield Ivy because of the shape of the leaves but in America as the Sweetheart Ivy from the supposedly heart-shaped leaves. A distinct variety it was a favourite of the late E. A. Bowles, a noted British horticulturist, and is sometimes called Bowles Shield Ivy. Synonyms include *Hedera hastata*, *H. helix cordata*, *H. helix ovata* and *H. helix* 'Sweetheart'; it has been confused with *H. helix* 'Scutifolia'.

The leaf characteristic, the overlapping of the two basal lobes is consistent on younger leaves but there appears to be no consistency in the method of lobe overlap, right over left or *vice versa*, varying from shoot to shoot and with individual leaves upon shoots. There is no reversion to the normal 'Ivy' leaf but the plant achieves arborescence and the consequent more simple rounded leaves fairly readily. Although a slow-growing variety, an ancient plant at Kew has reached the eaves of a two-storey building. The arborescent form is occasionally grown; there is a plant in Bowles Corner at the RHS Wisley Garden. A variegated form has not been recorded. Essentially a wall ivy, the plant has a quiet appeal In America the leaves are used in decoration on St Valentine's Day, most appropriate for the leaves are more heart-shaped than shield-like.

Habit   Vining.
Stems   Green, stout. Internodes 2–3 cm.
Petioles   Green.
Leaves   In outline three lobed but in fact the sinuses so shallow or absent as to make an unlobed deltoid, 6–10 cm by 8–10 cm. Leaf base strongly cordate with overlapping lobes. Leaf blade thick with smooth, well-defined edge. Dark green with purple tones in autumn. The veins, slightly lighter, are not prominent.

'DIGITATA'

This name is one of the earliest applied to an ivy variety. It was one of seven catalogued by the celebrated nurseryman, Conrad Loddiges of Hackney, London, in 1826 and was mentioned by the Edinburgh nurserymen, Peter Lawson & Sons, in their *Arboretum et Fruticetum* of 1846. The plant was described by Paul (1867), 'Leaves dark-green, long and pointed, broad at base deeply cleft, growth rapid. Shoots less numerous than in most others.' Nicholson (1885) illustrated the plant but, mistakenly I suggest, said it scarcely differed from 'Caenwoodiana'. Lawrence & Schulze (1942) give a detailed description and illustration of the plant and say that it was first recognised in Ireland, 'Made known by Mr Hodgens and noticed by Dr Mackay (*Flora Hibernica*, 1836)'. It was said to have been found growing wild near the former nursery gardens at Dungas Town, Wicklow and listed as *H. helix* 'Hodgensii' or *H. helix* 'Incisa'. If this were so Loddiges would seem to have had the variety before Mr Hodgens. I incline to the view that it is, in any event, one of the variations that may be found wild in Britain and it is possible that more than one person might come across this variant.

It is listed as one of three clones in a Digitata group by Nannenga-Bremekemp (1970) who draws attention to the leaves being wavy at the sinuses. Bean (1973) agrees with Lawrence & Schulze, suggesting that it is the same plant as 'Hodgensii' and notes its sharp forward-pointing lobes, narrow sinuses and the ray hairs more numerous than in most *helix* clones.

Comparisons of the clone 'Rottingdean', widely grown in Britain and Europe, suggest that this is in fact a clone of the digitata group; 'Rottingdean' was introduced by the late Roland Jackman, a keen-eyed plantsman who noticed the plant in the suburb of Rottingdean near Brighton in Sussex. Paul described a plant called Digitata Nova as being similar to Digitata but with smaller leaves. Possibly this clone, 'Digitata Nova' came into general circulation but stands of the original, larger-leaved Digitata persisted and it was one of these that Jackman spotted. This is speculation but it seems likely that 'Rottingdean' is in fact the original 'Digitata' and not a distinct clone; less worthy forms may well have circulated as 'Digitata' in the long period since 1826. Certainly the plant, after 150 years, remains an excellent wall ivy, hardy and with an interesting leaf.

Habit   Vining.
Stems   Green-purple. Internodes 2–4 cm.
Petioles Green-purple.
Leaves   Five lobed, 7–9 cm by 7–10 cm. Digitate, centre lobe a little longer than the two laterals, apices acute, the two basal lobes reduced, leaf base truncate. Sinuses narrow, convolute at clefts. Dark green, veins light but not prominent.

'DIREKTOR BADKE'

Charming and unusual, the leaves of this ivy sometimes seem to be made up of three circles, so rounded are the small, three-lobed leaves. The clone was selected by Hans Schmidt, nurseryman of Bockum-Hövel, Germany, and exhibited at BUGA, the large German flower show at Dortmund in 1960. The name commemorates Richard Badke, Director of the Gartenbauschule und Gärtnerischen Versuchsanstalt (Horticultural College and Gardens) at Wolbeck from 1930 until his death in 1956.

The clone is similar to 'Ralf' but has smaller, more rounded leaves. The compact growth and neat foliage make it a useful pot plant. A similar clone was later selected at the Stauss nurseries in Germany and named 'Christian'. This name was withdrawn when it was realised that the clone already existed and had been named.

Habit	Self-branching.
Stems	Red-purple. Internodes 1.5–2 cm.
Petioles	Green, pink at base.
Leaves	Three lobed, 1.5–2.5 cm by 3–3.5 cm. Lobes rounded and not pronounced, often merging to produce a rounded, deltoid leaf. Leaf base strongly cordate, basal lobes sometimes overlapping slightly. Soft light green with lighter veins. Centre vein occasionally turns red-purple in strong sun or in cold.

'DOMINO'

This clone, a mutation from 'Eugen Hahn', was selected by Gebr. Stauss of Möglingen near Stuttgart and named by them in 1979. In its fine mottle it is identical to 'Eugen Hahn' although the green appears a shade darker. The leaves instead of being heart-shaped and unlobed are typically ivy-shaped, five lobed but with the two basal lobes almost vestigial; like 'Eugen Hahn' it is an excellent plant for troughs or baskets.

Habit	Short jointed but throwing strong vining trails.
Stems	Purple. Internodes 1.5–5 cm.
Petioles	Green-purple.
Leaves	Strongly three lobed, 3–4 cm by 4–5 cm with two vestigial basal lobes. Centre lobe wedge-shaped. Lateral lobes bluntly acute, three-quarters the length of the centre lobe. Shallow sinus makes laterals unite almost at right angles to centre lobe. Ground colour cream, heavily spotted and marbled with slightly darker green than 'Eugen Hahn'.

'ERECTA'

The 'Transactions of the Royal Horticultural Society' for the year 1898 contain the report of a meeting of its Scientific Committee held on the 22 March of that year as follows:

Ivy Sports. Dr Masters exhibited sprays of a peculiar small leaved dwarf ivy remarkable for sending up vertical shoots with distichous leaves, though un-attached to a wall. The habit appears to have become fixed, even in free growing branches. On some shoots however, the leaves were spirally arranged as

Hedera canariensis 'Gloire de Marengo'

2   *Hedera canariensis* 'Margino maculata'

Hedera canariensis 'Ravensholst'

4   *Hedera colchica* 'Dentata'

Hedera colchica 'Dentata Variegata'

6   *Hedera colchica* 'Sulphur Heart'

7 *Hedera helix* 'Alt Heidelberg'

8 *Hedera helix* 'Angularis Aurea'

9 *Hedera helix* 'Anne Marie'

10 *Hedera helix* 'Ardingly'

11 *Hedera helix* 'Boskoop'

12 *Hedera helix* 'Buttercup'

13 *Hedera helix* 'Cavendishii'

14 *Hedera helix* 'Congesta'

15 *Hedera helix* 'Conglomerata'

16 *Hedera helix* 'Cuspidata Major'

17 *Hedera helix* 'Dealbata'

18 *Hedera helix* 'Deltoidea'

19 *Hedera helix* 'Domino'

20 *Hedera helix* 'Erecta'

21 *Hedera helix* 'Eva'

22 *Hedera helix* 'Fantasia'

23 *Hedera helix* 'Fluffy Ruffles'

24 *Hedera helix* 'Gavotte'

25   *Hedera helix* 'Glacier'

26   *Hedera helix* 'Goldheart'

27   *Hedera helix* 'Goldstern'

28   *Hedera helix* 'Green Ripple'

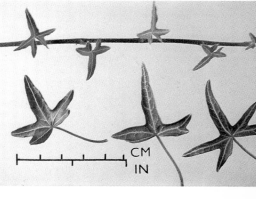

29   *Hedera helix* 'Harald'

30   *Hedera helix* 'Heron'

31 *Hedera helix* 'Hibernica Variegata'

32 *Hedera helix* 'Ivalace'

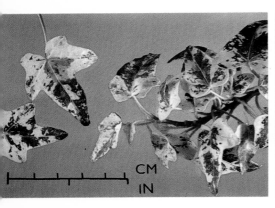

33 *Hedera helix* 'Kolibri'

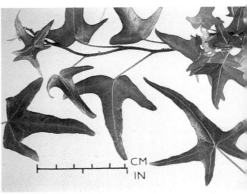

34 *Hedera helix* 'Königer's Auslese'

35 *Hedera helix* 'Little Diamond'

36 *Hedera helix* 'Minor Marmorata'

7 *Hedera helix* 'Neilson'

38 *Hedera helix* 'Parsley Crested'

9 *Hedera helix* 'Peter'

40 *Hedera helix* 'Professor Friedrich Tobler'

1 *Hedera helix* 'Ruche'

42 *Hedera helix* 'Sagittifolia'

43   *Hedera helix* 'Sagittifolia Variegata'   44   *Hedera helix* 'Shamrock'

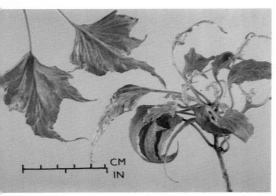

45   *Hedera helix* 'Spectre'   46   *Hedera helix* 'Spetchley'

47   *Hedera helix* 'Stift Neuburg'   48   *Hedera helix* 'Sulphurea'

49   *Hedera helix* 'Telecurl'

50   *Hedera helix* 'Triton'

51   *Hedera nepalensis*

52   *Hedera pastuchovii*

53   *Hedera rhombea*

54   *Hedera rhombea* 'Variegata'

55 *Hedera helix* 'Glacier', a foil for the berries of *Cotoneaster horizontalis*.

56 *Hedera canariensis* as ground-cover with contrasting paeony foliage.

57 *Hedera helix* 'Caenwoodiana Aurea' clothing a gate-pillar at Polesdon Lacey gardens, Surrey.

58 *Hedera helix* 'Erecta' as a rock-garden plant.

59 *Hedera helix* 'Goldheart' contrasts charmingly with these red roses.

60 *Hedera helix* 'Sagittifolia Variegata' adding colour to a low wall.

61 *Hedera colchica* 'Dentata Variegata' adding character to a modern house.

62 *Hedera canariensis* 'Sulphur Heart' making an attractive backcloth on a brick wall.

63 A planting of the adult form of *H. helix* 'Hibernica' provides an attractive shrub feature.

64 *Hedera helix* 'Hibernica'; a clipped hedge of the adult form makes an attractive surround to the Palm House at Kew Gardens, Surrey.

65 *Hedera helix* 'Congesta' the smaller leaved erect ivy as a rock-garden plant.

66   *Hedera canariensis* ground-cover for a sheltered situation.

67   *Hedera colchica* 'Dentata Variegata'; this striking ivy enhancing a flight of steps in Kew Gardens.

68   An ancient plant of *H. helix* 'Chrysophylla' combines with roses to make
a lovely picture on a gate-pillar in Oxford Botanic Garden.

69 *Hedera colchica* 'Dentata', the 'Ivy Wall' at Polesdon Lacey, Surrey, a National. Trust property.

70 *Hedera helix* 'Buttercup' contrasts beauti fully with Clematis 'Hagley Hybrid'.

71 The small-leaved *H. helix* 'Spetchley' makes ideal ground-cover for small bulbs.

is usual on such branches. It may be observed that the change from the distichous arrangement on the horizontal branches of the common Laurel to a spiral one when the boughs grow erect, is common, but it is not a fixed character.

This is the first reference to an upright ivy, unfortunately we do not know the source or nature of Dr Master's plant for we have inherited three distinct erect ivies, this one 'Erecta', 'Congesta' and 'Russelliana'. Hibberd did not mention an erect ivy in his book *The Ivy* (1872) nor in his account of the extensive collection in the Chiswick garden of the RHS (1889). In a period of intense interest in ivies one may assume that such a distinctive variety would not be overlooked so it seems certain that Dr Master's report was the approximate date of introduction. Its appearance in catalogues was much confused with 'Conglomerata'. The first catalogue reference is that of David Russell of Brentwood, Essex, in 1901, three years after Dr Master's report. They listed as *conglomerata*, 'Erect growing, very distinct', what I assume to be this plant while the creeping form they described as *'conglomerata prostrata* – a useful variety for the rock garden'. Thereafter various catalogues describe an erect-growing variety as *'Minima'*, *'conglomerata erecta'* or *'Congesta'*. The first authoritative description was that of Lawrence & Schulze (1942), forty-four years after Dr Master's find! They described the plant as *H. helix* 'Erecta' but the description and the illustration is more typical of the close-growing, sharp-leaved form which has acquired the name 'Congesta' on the Continent; because of its extensive use there I suggest it be retained for that form and that the name 'Erecta' apply to the form described here which has larger leaves and thicker, lighter-coloured stems. This form, incidentally, is more common in British gardens while plants from the Continent are usually the thinner-stemmed, sharper-leaved 'Congesta'. In Britain both forms may be seen in the Oxford Botanic Garden and the Royal Horticultural Society's Garden at Wisley. 'Erecta' is stronger growing, a coarser plant generally, suited to the bigger rock garden and for shady places; 'Congesta' is more suitable for the smaller situation. Both are plants of great architectural value, they can never be confused with 'Conglomerata' since they resolutely refuse to climb, however closely planted to walls.

97

Habit	Non-climbing, erect.
Stems	Short jointed, green, freely producing adventitious roots. Internodes, 1 cm.
Petioles	Light green.
Leaves	Three lobed, very occasionally unlobed, 4–6 cm by 4–6 cm. In two ranks, the distichous arrangement less noticeable in older shoots. Leaf sinuses usually shallow, centre lobe slightly longer than laterals. Apices bluntly acute. Dark green, veins light green to grey.

'EUGEN HAHN'

According to Krussman (*Handbuch der Laubgeholze*, 1977) this was a mutation from 'Pennsylvanian'. There is no plant of that name in the American Ivy Society 'Preliminary Check-list' nor in other available lists and I suspect the parent variety to be 'Sylvanian' (US Patent variety 430 of October 1940). The similarity of the leaves to 'Sylvanian' is mentioned by Brother Heieck in his check-list of the clones grown by Gebr. Stauss and in fact the clone was introduced by them at the BUGA Horticultural Show of 1977 and described in 'Gartenwelt' (October 1977). Brother Heieck's description of 'Leaves dappled and speckled with light-green, dark-green, grey-green and white to yellowish white distributed in large or small patches over the whole leaf', can hardly be bettered.

The powdered 'Pepper and Salt' effect may not be to everyone's taste but it is certainly distinct. A vining clone producing fairly compact trails it is useful for decoration, particularly troughs and baskets. The newer introduction 'Domino' a mutation from 'Eugen Hahn' selected by Gebr. Stauss may, however, well supplant it.

Habit	Short jointed but throwing strong vining trails.
Stems	Purple. Internodes 1.5–3 cm.
Petioles	Green-purple, rarely more than 2 cm.
Leaves	Remotely three lobed, more often unlobed with frequently a lobe-like protusion to one side of the leaf base. Heart-shaped to triangular, 3–4 cm by 3–5 cm wide, noticeably thin. Base colour cream, densely stippled and marbled with medium green.

The first record of this popular clone is in *Gartenwelt und Zierpflan-zenbau* (1966), where it appears that Tage Melin of Hjallese, Denmark, in the early 1960s selected it from the clone 'Harald'. Large quantities are grown at the present time for the house-plant trade because growth is rapid and the small leaves make it suitable for pot work and particularly for bottle gardens. In common with 'Harald' it has proved reasonably hardy in Britain, albeit with some damage to the variegated leaf portions in frost and cold winds. On the Continent it is considered an indoor plant and its USA limit is probably Zone 8. It is described by Nannenga-Bremekamp (1970) as 'Pittsburgh Variegated'. In America, Schaepman has pointed out that the white or parti-white leaves show green veins when in low light situations. Reversion to totally green leaves occurs occasionally: these can be identified as 'Pittsburgh' and one may assume that this clone and 'Harald' are variations of 'Pittsburgh Variegated' described by Bates ('The National Horticultural Magazine') in America as long ago as 1940. Although 'Eva' is listed in the American Ivy Society Check-list, the American writer Suzanne Pierot makes no mention of it in her *Ivy Book*; presumably it is less grown in America than in Europe.

Habit	Self-branching.
Stems	Green-purple. Internodes 2–3 cm.
Petioles	Green-purple.
Leaves	Three lobed, 2.5–3 cm by 2.5–3.5 cm. Centre lobe usually acuminate and up to twice the length of laterals. Sinuses shallow, lateral lobes often wedge-shaped, centre lobe occasionally so. Colour, grey-green irregular centre, blotched darker green, bordered with cream-white, this extending sometimes to half the leaf. Veins light green.

'FAN'

An interesting ivy whose name indicates the shape of its leaves and their radiating veins. It has been described as 'Crenata' (Nannenga-Bremekamp, 1970), a synonym queried by Heieck (1977), and in the American-Ivy Society Check-list (1975). Certainly it is not 'Crenata'; this was a vining type variety first described by Paul

(1867) and illustrated by Hibberd (1872). 'Fan' throws out short vining trails with a cluster of small leaves at virtually every node, a characteristic of modern self-branching clones but not mentioned or depicted in 'Crenata' by the early writers. The short fat-lobed leaves of 'Fan' are a soft apple-green. Its close habit makes it a good pot or trough plant.

Habit   Self-branching with short trails.
Stems   Purple-green. Internodes 3.5–4 cm. Miniature shoots with leaf clusters at every node.
Petioles Pink-green.
Leaves   Five lobed, 3–4.5 cm by 5–7 cm. Lobes often reduced to forward-pointing protrusions. Apices blunt, leaf base truncate to acute. Soft apple-green, veins prominently raised radiating fan-like from the petiole.

'FANTASIA'

A yellow-cream mottled clone that has also appeared as 'Aalsmeer' and 'Pittsburgh Variegated'. The variegation can be so extreme as to produce almost white leaves. Probably best as an indoor plant. When planted outside in Britain it survives hard winters but with severe damage to variegated areas and a marked tendency to green reversion.

Habit   Self-branching.
Stems   Pink-purple. Internodes 1.5–2 cm.
Petioles Green-pink.
Leaves   Five lobed, 3–4 cm by 4–6 cm. Apices acute, sinuses wide, leaf base deeply cordate. Basic colour bright-green heavily mottled yellow-cream. Veins light green.

'FLAVESCENS'

Identification of this clone has been very dependent on nursery catalogues, particularly those of L. R. Russell Ltd, now of Windlesham, Surrey. The descriptions dating from 1901 to 1932 refer variously to 'Lasting golden foliage', 'Small bright yellow foliage which retains its bright colour permanently' and 'Slow growing, foliage entirely bright gold'. The firm no longer stock 'Flavescens' but in summary these descriptions fit the ivy still occasionally found in gardens and include the plant growing on the 'Ivy Wall' at Kew and recorded there as 'Flavescens'. The only firm apart from Russells to have listed the plant in Britain appeared to be Gauntletts of Chiddingfold in Surrey. In 1865 the German firm of Haage & Schmidt, noted for its ivy introductions, listed a variety as 'Flava' described as, 'With small yellow mottled variegated leaves'. 'Flavescens' shows no mottling or variegation and the Haage & Schmidt plant may well have been 'Nigra Aurea'.

The leaves of 'Flavescens' differ from other 'golden' ivies in being of a uniform pale yellow-green. Leaves that are fully exposed to the light take on a deeper yellow but the plant lacks really green or even parti-green leaves. Slow growing and maintaining its yellow colour consistently the arborescent form, which appears most common, presents a mass of fairly small, evenly pointed, elliptic yellow leaves. In this state it was obviously a favourite for 'Bedding out' and 'Yellow gardens' in the pre-1914 days.

Habit	Vining.
Stems	Green-yellow. Internodes 2.5–3 cm.
Petioles	Green-yellow.
Leaves	Three lobed, 3–4 cm by 3–4 cm. The lobes not prominent but showing more as protrusions on the small leaves. Leaf base slightly cordate. Colour very light green to clear yellow. Veins not prominent.

'FLUFFY RUFFLES'

A most distinctive ivy of whose origin little seems to be known save that it is American. It was listed in Graf's *Exotica* in 1963 and described in *The Ivy Book* (1974) by Suzanne Pierot.

Looking at this plant it is difficult to believe it to be an ivy. The leaves are deeply waved and convoluted and because the lobes almost encircle the petiole, appear almost like pom-pons. Definitely an indoor ivy and highly suitable as a specimen pot plant, it is a most attractive plant for the ivy enthusiast and a talking point as a most 'un-ivy-like' ivy.

Habit	Branching, open growth.
Stems	Green-purple. Internodes 2–3 cm.
Petioles	Long and slender, green-pink.

Leaves	Basically five lobed, but so convoluted as to appear like frilled circular rosettes, 4–6 cm by 4–6 cm. Leaf base strongly auriculate so as to appear almost circular. Strongly veined, veins radiate from the petiole/leaf-blade junction, light to yellow-green. Leaf blade mid-green.

'GARLAND'

The first description of this clone appeared in an article by Bess L. Shippy 'English Ivy Keeps Changing Faces' in the American publication 'Flower Grower' in September 1955. From this it appeared that Carl Frey of Lima, Ohio, discovered the clone as a mutation of 'Pittsburgh' in 1945. The plant is described by Graf (1963), Pierot (1974) and in the American Ivy Society's Bulletin (No. 4, 1978).

All descriptions agree in emphasising its compact bushy habit, variable leaves and their close setting like 'wide plaited garlands' to quote Bess Shippy. The AIS report it as standing − 12°C (10°F) and suggest it as ground cover for Zone 7 areas or warmer; it has proved hardy in Britain. A good easy pot plant but also ground cover for small areas.

Habit	Compact and bushy.
Stems	Green-pink. Internodes 1–3 cm.
Petioles	Green-pink.
Leaves	Sometimes three lobed but often unlobed and ovate, 5–6 cm by 4–5 cm. Leaf blade slightly folded at leaf-blade/petiole junction and waved. There is a distinct downward dip in the main lobe. The leaves are closely set on the stem, bright green with lighter green, well-defined veins.

'GAVOTTE'

This ivy is often confused with 'Brokamp' although the two clones arose as mutations from completely different varieties. The history of 'Gavotte', however, is well documented. It was selected by Harry van de Laar in Boskoop, Holland, in 1953 from the American variety 'Star' and introduced commercially in Holland in 1956; Van de Laar's description is in 'Vakblad voor de Bloemisterij' –

May 1965. Krussman in his *Handbuch der Laubgeholze* – 1977 lists 'Gavotte' but mistakenly attributes it to the Brokamp Nursery.

The leaf of 'Gavotte' is slightly more linear than that of 'Brokamp' and possibly less auriculate at the leaf base. For all practical purposes they are the same and the comments made in respect of 'Brokamp' apply to this plant, namely it is an interesting and useful clone for hanging baskets and ground cover for small areas.

Habit	Self-branching but with long trails.
Stems	Green-purple. Internodes 1.5–3 cm.
Petioles	Green, 0.5–2 cm.
Leaves	Mostly entire and lanceolate-linear, acuminate. Occasional lobed to heart-shaped leaves, 5 cm long by 1–1.5 cm wide. Central vein not unduly prominent. Medium green to a much lighter green in summer.

'GLACIER'

One of the most popular ivies for house-plant work. At the present time millions of this silver grey-leaved clone are raised annually in Europe and America. Although popular since World War 2 and widely grown, little seems known of its origins; certainly in 1950 it was being grown by Weber in California and was introduced into Germany by 1954. Lawrence (1956) grouped it with 'Cavendishii' but to me it has little or no affinity with that ivy. Nannenga-Bremekamp described it (1970) and this appears to be the first official recognition. In Britain it is fairly hardy and outside makes an excellent grey foil for colourful shrubs or plants. Probably hardy in USA Zone 7, Suzanne Pierot says it is hardy outdoors south of New Jersey. When grown outside, leaves can become much larger and more irregular.

Habit	Vining and slightly branching.
Stems	Purple-green. Internodes 2–4 cm.
Petioles	Green, tinged purple.
Leaves	Three to five lobed, basal lobes little more than projections 3–6 cm by 3–5 cm. Sinuses so shallow as to make the leaf triangular or three lobed. Leaf base cordate. Ground colour grey-green with lighter silver-grey patches, occasionally a thin cream rim.

The winter leaves, glossy purple, veined light green make this an ideal flower arranger's ivy. That early connoisseur of ivies, William Paul, described it in the 'Gardener's Chronicle' of 1867 as 'Leaves pale green, of medium size, almost entire; very glossy looking as if varnished. Growth very rapid, forming masses of foliage'. Who was Glym? We don't know; Nicholson (1885) and one or two nineteenth-century catalogues refer to it as Glym's Ivy but to date I can trace no nursery or horticultural person of that name. Following Paul's description it was occasionally catalogued, increasingly so after about 1880. Hibberd (1872) described it, but on the slender pretext of a slight twisting of the leaves in winter, named it 'Tortuosa'. In 1889 it received a First Class Certificate in the Royal Horticultural Society's Trial of Ivies at Chiswick. When reporting on the ivies grown in the Society's gardens (RHS Journal, 1890) Hibberd described it as 'Tortuosa' adding a footnote that it was 'Submitted by Mr Fraser as Glymii'. Since then it has sometimes circulated, erroneously, as 'Scutifolia' and 'Linsii'. Hibberd's appellation of 'Tortuosa' received little support and Mr Glym's name is still honoured by a most useful climbing ivy. Because of its gloss it is the best of the purple ivies; Nicholson suggested it as suitable for pot culture; it is a vigorous grower and one would need very large pots, possible probably in 1885; nowadays I think it is better as a wall ivy or in its adult form as a bush.

Habit	Vining.
Stems	Green in summer to purple in winter. Internodes 2–4 cm.
Petioles	As stems.
Leaves	Remotely three lobed, short, 4–5 cm by 5–6 cm. Sinus virtually absent. Centre lobe acute and short. Leaf base truncate, sides of the leaf tend to be straight, i.e. parallel with the centre vein. Deep green with a very glossy upper surface. Veins lighter but not prominent until winter when they stand out against the deep purple of the leaf blade.

'GOLDCHILD'

Ivies are usually easy of cultivation. This attractive clone is possibly the exception that proves the rule. It is a rather weak grower, intolerant of under- or over-watering. These limitations have not endeared it to the mass-producers of house plants; indeed at the time of writing Fibrex Nurseries Ltd, of Evesham, Gloucestershire is the only nursery listing it.

The origin of the clone is not known; it was acquired by Thomas Rochford Ltd of Hertfordshire among a collection of house plants purchased from a continental supplier. The name 'Goldchild' was proposed to Mr Rochford Snr. and under that name it was exhibited at the Royal Horticultural Society's show on 16 November 1971 and received an Award of Merit. 'Goldchild' is not generally hardy in Britain but carefully grown is an attractive pot-plant ivy. A similar plant has circulated as 'Golden Chicago'.

Habit	Self-branching.
Stems	Purple-green. Internodes 1.5–2 cm.
Petioles	Purple-green.
Leaves	Three lobed, 3–4 cm by 4–5 cm. Centre lobe wedge-shaped, sinuses shallow, occasional vestigial basal lobes. Leaf blade slightly cordate. The yellow leaf margin completely surrounds a central area of grey-green. Leaf slightly cupped but generally little distortion, veins light grey-green.

'GOLDCRAFT'

Unlike so many ivies the history of this useful clone is well documented. Thought to be a mutation of the common ivy it was found in 1969 by Mr Curren Craft Jnr., of Cayce, South Carolina, and named 'Craft's Golden'. Later, with the raiser's approval, it was introduced and named 'Goldcraft' by Mr W. O. Freeland of Columbia. The clone was registered in 1976 with the American Ivy Society who operate the International Register of *Hedera* Names, as 'Goldcraft' (Reg. 761). It is one of the few yellow-leaved ivies and has a green splash in the leaf centre. It is deemed hardy in USA Zones 8 and possibly 7 but while it would probably succeed in sheltered parts of Britain it is more suitable and very attractive for pot culture or hanging baskets. It appears to be a better grower than 'Goldchild' but the yellow colour of the latter is more defined and persistent.

Habit	Self-branching with short trails.
Stems	Green. Internodes 1.5–3 cm.
Petioles	Green.
Leaves	Three lobed, 3–4 cm by 3–4 cm. Centre lobe broad wedge-shaped, lateral lobes short, quarter length of centre lobe. Sinuses shallow, apices acute. Lime-yellow with green 'splash' irregularly placed. Leaves darken with age, veins light green, not pronounced.

'GOLDHEART'

One of the best vining ivies ever introduced, the red-pink of the young stems and dark-green leaves splashed in the centre with clear yellow, combine to make a superb picture. Essentially a wall ivy it is occasionally grown as a pot plant on moss-sticks but does not fill in sufficiently for it to be recommended for that purpose. It is not suitable for ground cover, tending to produce all-green leaves when on the ground. Colour is usually well maintained on wall plants but it is worthwhile to cut out any all-green shoots when they appear. It is hardy in Britain, and probably in most of Europe and reportedly grows well in the USA as far north as Zone 7.

The origin of the plant is not certain. It first appeared in Italian plant catalogues in the 1950s as 'Oro del Bogliasco' (Bogliasco Gold), apparently having originated in a nursery near Bogliasco, a town east of Genoa on the Italian Riviera. It made its way to Holland in 1955 and to Britain and was exhibited at the Royal Horticultural Society's show on 18 May 1970 as 'Jubilee' and received an Award of Merit. Shortly afterwards it was realised that the name 'Jubilee' had been given by Hesse of Weener, Hanover, in 1907 to a distinct white-edged variety and furthermore that the plant exhibited had been listed in Holland by van de Laar in 1965 as 'Goldhertz'. The exhibiting firm, L. R. Russell Ltd, accordingly named their plant 'Goldheart' and a note to that effect was published in the 'Proceedings of the Royal Horticultural Society' (Vol. 95, 1970, p. 63). It is still listed in most Italian and many European catalogues as 'Oro del Bogliasco'. An early description was that in the catalogue of Baldacci & Sons, Pistoia, Italy in 1963, ' "Oro del Bogliasco" – Leaves the same size as those of *helix*, colour a fine deep yellow streaked with green in the middle. Quick growing, it clings well both to walls and to other supports.' The plant having been listed by van de Laar in 1965 as 'Goldhertz' was described as 'Goldheart' by Nannenga-Bremekamp (1970) and Bean (1973). In Baldacci's catalogue description the leaf colours are curiously transposed, in fact the yellow splash is of course surrounded by green. Despite the priority of the Italian name, the vagueness of the catalogue descriptions, followed by the accurate descriptions of Nannenga-Bremekamp and Bean and subsequently that in the American Ivy Society Bulletin (Summer 1975) suggest that the name 'Goldheart' should stand. Although van de Laar listed the plant as 'Goldhertz' in 1965 I can find no record of award or description under that name whereas, as mentioned above, the plant gained an Award of Merit as 'Goldheart'. The names 'Oro del Bogliasco', 'Goldhertz' and 'Golden Jubilee' remain as synonyms; 'Jubilee' and 'Jubilaum' are incorrect since they belong to another plant.

The reversion to green has been selected by Freeland in America and named by him 'Teena'. Assuming this to be the usual and all-too-common reversion I would regard it as an unnecessary name. All the indications are that 'Goldheart' was a mutation of *helix* and that the reverted leaves are *helix*.

Habit	Vining.
Stems	Pink-red, browning with age. Internodes 2–3 cm.
Petioles	Mostly pink, occasionally light green or yellow.
Leaves	Three lobed, 4–6 cm by 4–6 cm. Centre lobe longest and acuminate, lateral lobes bluntly acute, vestigial basal lobes sometimes apparent, leaf base truncate. Colour dark green, irregularly splashed, almost always centrally clear yellow. Veins not prominent.

'GOLDSTERN'

This is a striking arrow-head-leaved counterpart of 'Goldcraft'. It has the same lime-green colour but in this case a consistent darker green central splash. Like 'Goldcraft' the leaf darkens with age. The clone was selected by Brother Heieck at Neuburg Monastery near Heidelberg from 'Star' and named by him in 1979. The thin, well-defined arrow-head leaves with their lime-green colour makes this a most useful pot plant but its light colour and contrasting green splash are not sufficiently marked to be appreciated in outdoor situations.

Habit	Self-branching and compact.
Stems	Green-light purple. Internodes 1–2 cm.
Petioles	Green-pink.
Leaves	Five lobed, 3.5–5 cm by 4.5–6 cm. Centre lobe prolonged to twice the length of the two laterals which stand at right angles to it, apices acuminate. The two basal lobes are small and back-pointing. Lime-green with a darker green splash in or around the leaf centre.

'GRACILIS'

First described by Hibberd in the *Floral World* (1864) no synonyms were given and one may assume this was a name Hibberd gave to an ivy grown in his day but un-named. The plant began to appear in catalogues: Hendersons of London listed it in 1865 as slender branched; William Cibran & Son of Altrincham, Cheshire, in 1894 described it as a 'Small cut leaved variety veined rich bronze in autumn'. In the Royal Horticultural Society's Trial of Ivies in 1889 the variety received an Award of Merit and Hibberd in his report on ivies growing in the Society's garden (1890) described it thus, 'Gracilis has a singularly elegant appearance. It is a minor *helix* of wiry habit with purple stems and leaf stalks; the leaves conspicuously veined. An excellent rockery plant.' Nicholson (1885) wrote 'H h gracilis [slender] leaves usually three-lobed colour rather light dull green, richly bronzed in autumn. Stems wiry, purplish. A very pretty variety for covering a wall or a tree stump.' The latest (8th) edition of Bean (1973) follows Nicholson. Graff (1963) linked it with the 'Ramosa complex such as *H h* "Pittsburgh"'. I suggest this is mistaken; leaf size may be similar but the plant appears different in every other way. Nannenga-Bremekamp (1970) illustrates and describes 'Gracilis' but the plant does not seem to match the cut-leaved and wiry growth of Hibberd and the early catalogues. What I believe to be the true 'Gracilis' is listed by Hillier & Sons (Winchester) and Fibrex Nurseries Ltd (Evesham) and as in Hibberd's day can be recommended as a 'pretty' ivy, too loose and spreading for ground cover but good for covering tree stumps and for large walls. It is as hardy as *helix* of which it is a leaf variant.

Habit	Vining with long spreading trails.
Stems	Purple. Internodes 3–6 cm.
Petioles	Purple.
Leaves	Three and five lobed, 2–4 cm by 3–4 cm. Leaf base truncate to cordate. Lobes wedge-shaped, acute, centre lobe only slightly longer than laterals. Sinuses generally shallow, margin slightly convolute at cleft. Colour deep green, veins light green.

'GREEN FEATHER'

A classic mutation and the forerunner of many interesting clones, this was spotted by Mr Meagher an employee on the nursery of Mr Fred Danker of Albany, New York, who in 1939 introduced it to the trade, honouring his employee by giving it the unpublished name of 'Meagheri'. Bates, writing in the American 'National Horticultural Magazine' in October 1940, described the plant under the name 'Green Feather'. This was an authentic publication and although Lawrence & Schulze (1942) rejected Bates' name and described the plant as 'Meagheri', the first published name has priority. Nannenga-Bremekamp (1970) and the American Ivy Society (Preliminary Check-list of Cultivated Hedera) both support the first validly published name.

Over the years the clone appears to have changed; plants now in circulation do not show the extremely short internodes of 3 mm quoted by Bates, or the smallness of leaf that he suggested. The plant nevertheless remains a most useful pot plant, excellent for hanging baskets and low wall cover. It is still often listed as 'Meagheri' and sometimes 'Megheri'.

Habit	Vining, moderately self-branching.
Stems	Purple-green. Internodes 1–3 cm.
Petioles	Purple-green.
Leaves	Three lobed, 3–5 cm by 3–4 cm. Sinuses narrow, occasionally split almost as far as the vein. Centre lobe long, acuminate to cuspidate. Lateral lobes bluntly acute and sometimes slightly folded upwards. Dark green, veins lighter green, the purple of the petiole occasionally seen

at the lower end of veins on upper surface but never on the under surface.

'GREEN FINGER'

This close-growing bright little ivy has several good points not least of which for the ivy enthusiast, anxious to make sure he has the correct clone, is the useful diagnostic fact that some leaves have a small heel-like projection at the leaf base. 'Green Finger' was found as a mutation of 'Star' by Mr W. O. Freeland at his nursery in Columbia, South Carolina ('American Hort. Mag.', 1971). In Britain the name has been erroneously applied to the very different clone Professor Friedrich Tobler'. The plant's stems are slender but closely set with deep-green, sharply pointed Bird's Foot type leaves. It has proved reasonably hardy in Britain and probably survives outdoors in USA Zone 7; it can be used as ground cover for small bulbs and the like on rock gardens but its prime use and value is as an indoor plant for pots, troughs or baskets.

Habit   Compact self-branching.
Stems   Purple. Internodes 1–1.5 cm.
Petioles Green-purple.
Leaves   Five lobed, 2–3.5 cm by 1–4 cm, but variability some-
          times produces three-, two- or even single-lobed leaves.
          Centre lobe prolonged and narrow (0.5–1 cm), apices
          acuminate, sinuses shallow, basal lobes, where present,
          back pointing. Some leaves carry a heel-like projection
          at the base of one of the lateral lobes. Dark green, three
          main veins prominent.

'GREEN RIPPLE'

It is said that 'Good wine needs no bush': in other words a good article does not need advertising; it sells itself. This is true, but a good article with a good name is a winner. This is so of 'Green Ripple', an inspired name which well describes the rippling green of the strongly veined leaves.

'Green Ripple' was a mutation from 'Maple Queen' discovered in 1939 by Louis Hahn of Pittsburgh, Pennsylvania, and introduced by him. The plant was very well described by Bess L. Shippy as 'Green Ripple' in 'The Flower Grower', November 1950, and again in the same magazine in September 1955. In Holland, Harry van de Laar described it in 1965 as ' "Hahn's Green Ripple" imported from America in 1952' while Nannenga-Bremekamp (1970) using the same name, grouped it with 'Green Feather' and 'Shamrock'. The first name given, i.e. 'Green Ripple', is, however, the correct name. A well-established clone, it has proved its worth in various situations; as a pot plant it vines and branches sufficiently to cover moss-sticks or canes, or to furnish hanging baskets. It is a reasonable wall plant though tending to show reversion over a period. It makes good ground cover and is hardier than might be expected. The American Ivy Society suggest it is a possibility for USA Zone 5.

Habit	Vining but branching well.
Stems	Green-purple. Internodes 2–3 cm.
Petioles	Green-purple.
Leaves	Five-lobed, 5–10 cm by 5–7 cm. Lobes forward pointing, acuminate, sinuses shallow, margin at the cleft raised in an upward pleat. Leaf base cordate. Veins prominent on the leaf surface, pale green. Leaf colour bright deep green.

'HARALD'

As 'Harold', 'Herold' or 'Harald' this ivy is widely grown for the European pot-plant trade, indeed with 'Eva' and 'Anna Marie' it accounts for the bulk of the trade in variegated *helix* ivies at the present time. It was grown in 1958/9 in Denmark but its origin seems vague. Nannenga-Bremekamp (1970) suggests that it is synonymous with 'Cavendishii'; old plants of 'Cavendishii' are in existence in Britain and these, and material of that name circulating in British nurseries, bear no resemblance to this self-branching clone. Heieck (1977) points out that on the Stauss Ivy Nurseries near Heidelberg this clone has been selected out of 'Eva' suggesting, since 'Harald' is the older, that 'Eva' was a mutation from 'Harald'. I have seen 'Eva' revert back to 'Pittsburgh' and assume it to be a variation of 'Pittsburgh Variegated'. The description of 'Harald' by Brother Heieck appears to be the first botanically detailed note and his plant certainly the same as that listed as 'Harald' by Koch (*Gartenwelt*, 1972) and in the American Ivy Society's 'Preliminary Check-list' and circulating in Britain and listed in various catalogues. Synonyms include 'Anne Borch', 'Chicago Variegated', 'Ingrid' and 'Hahni'. In leaf size it is mid-way between 'Eva' and 'Anna Marie'.

Habit	Self-branching.
Stems	Green-purple. Internodes 2–4 cm.
Petioles	Green-purple.
Leaves	Three lobed with occasionally vestigial basal lobes. 4–6 cm by 4–5 cm. Lobes wedge-shaped, rounded or bluntly acute, sinuses shallow. Leaf base truncate or slightly cordate. Central portion grey-green, bordered irregularly with cream-white sometimes extending into a larger area. Veins light green, not prominent.

'HAZEL'

A mutation from 'Adam' selected by Thomas Rochford & Sons Ltd, of Broxbourne, England, around 1975 and named by them to mark the contributions to ivy cultivation of Mrs Hazel Key of Fibrex Nurseries, Evesham. The cream-white leaves, speckled and marbled green, resemble 'Kolibri' in colour but are broader and shorter. Like 'Kolibri' it is very much an ivy for indoors where dull light conditions seem to enhance the colour pattern.

Habit	Self-branching.
Stems	Green-pink. Internodes 1.5–2 cm.
Petioles	Green-pink.
Leaves	Three lobed, 2.5–3 cm by 2.5–4 cm, with two vestigial basal lobes. Centre lobe twice as long as laterals, apices acute, leaf base cordate. Basic colour cream-white substantially covered with grey-green having darker green patches upon it. Some leaves have only scattered areas of green. Veins cream, not pronounced.

'HEISE'

Often called 'Heise Denmark', this indicates its country of origin. It has been in cultivation for some time: Graf (1963) recorded it and Pierot (1974) points out that while the colour is similar to 'Glacier' the leaves are broader and the plant bushier. Very suitable for the pot-plant trade it has been propagated on a large scale and there are several forms in circulation. The following description is reckoned as typical.

Habit   Self-branching, compact.
Stems   Green-purple. Internodes 2–3.5 cm.
Petioles   Green.
Leaves   Three lobed, 3–4 cm by 3–5 cm. Apices acute, base slightly cordate, grey-green variegated cream.

'HELFORD RIVER'

The following description appears in Bean's *Trees and Shrubs Hardy in the British Isles* (1973).

> *Hedera helix* cv 'Helford River'. A large-leaved ivy found growing wild near the Helford Estuary by George Nicholson, Curator of Kew, in 1890 and introduced by him to the collection where it still grows. The leaves are conspicuously white-veined, variable in shape but mostly with a long central lobe and two backward spreading laterals.

The variety was recorded as 'Helfordiensis' in the Kew Hand List (1925). It is not mentioned in Tobler's 'Die Gattung Hedera' of 1912 but is listed in his 'Die Gartenformen der Gattung Hedera' of 1927. The name has been associated with the purple-leaved clones 'Woeneri' and 'Purpurea' but there is no apparent reason for this as the variety does not colour at all. Bean's description appears to be the first published and 'Helford River' to be the correct and most suitable name. A vigorous climber the grey-veined leaves provide contrast to other ivies; can be used for ground cover.

Habit   Vining.
Stems   Green-purple. Internodes 2–3 cm.
Petioles   Green-purple.
Leaves   Five lobed, 6–10 cm by 7–11 cm. Centre lobe prolonged and acuminate, lateral lobes wedge-shaped and acute, basal lobes back-pointing. Sinuses shallow. Medium green, veins show up strongly grey-white giving the impression of a greyish leaf.

113

In the late 1950s Roland Jackman of Woking, Surrey, found and named this selection of 'Pedata'. Similar in habit and colour it differs in its attenuated leaves, long internodes and wiry habit; indeed the small narrow-lobed leaves on the younger shoots look almost like the barbs on barbed wire. More interesting than beautiful it shows to best effect against a white wall or in a situation where its long stems can hang over a wall or bank; it can be grown into a wiry tangle on a lattice of wood or wire.

Habit   Vining, extending rapidly.
Stems   Grey-green. Internodes 3–6 cm.
Petioles   Generally short, 1–3 cm, dull-purple.
Leaves   Five lobed, basal lobes back pointing. 3–5 cm by 4–5 cm. Centre lobe one and a half times the length of the lateral lobes. Sinuses very shallow, in extreme cases the lateral lobes are at right angles to the centre lobe. Leaf blades attenuated sometimes almost to the veins. Dark grey-green, veins green-white.

'HIBERNICA'

Probably the most widely planted of all ivies, controversy as to its origin and identity has continued in horticultural circles for something like 140 years. The first recorded reference is that of George Lindley, a nurseryman of Catton near Norwich, England, who in 1815 listed three varieties in his catalogue: Common Ivy, the 'Striped' ivy and 'Hibernica', but without any descriptions. Later in 1836 Mackay wrote in his *Flora Hibernica*, 'A variety called the Irish ivy (of which I have specimens collected by Mr W. H. Andrews on the rocks at Ballybunian, County of Kerry) is much cultivated on account of its very large leaves and quick growth.' From this we may turn to the most recent comment, that in the 8th Edition of Bean's *Trees and Shrubs Hardy in the British Isles* (1973) '*H. helix* "Hibernica" '. A tetraploid variant of the common ivy with dull green leaves 3 to 6 inches across with usually five triangular lobes, the terminal one the largest.' In the intervening 137 years discussion as to its identity produced the following nomenclatural vicissitudes:

Hedera helix hibernica (Kirchn, Petzold & Kirchn) 1864.
H. Hibernica Scotica (Seeman, 'Journal of Botany') 1865.
H. Canariensis (Paul, 'Gardener's Chronicle') 1868.
H. grandifolia (syn, vegeta) (Hibberd, *The Ivy*) 1872.
H. Hibernica (Carrière, 'Revue Horticole') 1890.
H. helix Europea (Voss, 'Vilmorin Blumengartneri') 1896.
H. scotica (Chevalier, 'Monde Plante') 1933.

The origin of the plant may be doubtful but its value in the garden is certain. As long ago as 1868, M. Delchevalerie, Chef de Culture au Fleuriste de la Ville de Paris, wrote on the virtues of 'Le Lierre d'Irlande' for use in the squares and beds of Paris. His recommendation can be seen to this day on the Boulevards and the squares and cemeteries of Paris. In the celebrated 'Cimetiére du Père-Lachaise', the élite of France, from Chopin and Maréchal Ney to Edith Piaf, rest, surrounded by stone and 'Hibernica'. Paris was not alone in favouring this effective ground cover; many European cities and towns contain examples of its value as an unobtrusive background to architectural splendours or follies and its wide use in the eastern part of the USA, although a non-indigenous plant, demonstrates its versatility.

On walls or as ground cover it benefits from annual clipping. In its adult or arborescent form it can make an effective hedge. Few of the many thousands who visit the Royal Botanic Gardens at Kew realise that what appears to be a low covered wall surrounding the Palm House is in fact close-planted, arborescent 'Hibernica' clipped in hedge fashion. In Britain there can be few churchyards, parks or stately homes where the unmistakable large, slightly upward folded, dull-green leaves of 'Hibernica' do not provide cover or background. It has another attribute, being one of the parents of that very useful garden plant, the bi-generic × *Fatshedera lizei*, the other parent being *Fatsia japonica*.

Habit	Vining and vigorous.
Stems	Green. Internodes 5–7 cm.
Petioles	Green-purple.
Leaves	Five lobed, 5–9 cm by 8–14 cm. Lobes triangular and bluntly acute, centre lobe large and more prominent, sinuses shallow. Leaf base cordate. Dull matt-green, veins light grey-green not unduly prominent.

This clone appears to me to be a variation of 'Hibernica' and for convenience is placed here. Argument as to the origin and proper designation of *H. helix* 'Hibernica' has gone on for years and will probably continue. In this book I have accepted it as a tetraploid variety of *helix* and have pointed out its virtues and extensive use in city plantings. Whatever its origins it has in general remained remarkably consistent as regards leaf shape; of the few leaf variations in existence this one is probably the most useful horticulturally.

In essence it has the same slightly 'fluted' leaf as 'Hibernica' and certainly the same vigour but differs in having cuspid lobes and a slightly thickened leaf edge giving the leaf a 'sculptural' appearance with almost the solidity of a fatshedera. The petioles are very light green, lacking the slight tinge of red usually present in 'Hibernica'. It is hardy and will thrive in the same situations as 'Hibernica'.

'Hamilton' was introduced by Mrs Hazel Key of Fibrex Nurseries Ltd, Evesham, England, the name given being that of premises upon which it was found. It is hardy, a vigorous climbing and ground-cover ivy whose leaf variation makes it a useful alternative to the usual 'Hibernica'.

Habit	Vining.
Stems	Green. Internodes 3–5 cm.
Petioles	Light green.
Leaves	Five lobed, 6–7 cm by 9–10 cm. Lobes cuspid, centre lobe only slightly longer than laterals. The two basal lobes reduced to about one-third of laterals. Sinuses deep with convolution at the cleft. Distinctive thickened leaf edge giving a 'rimmed' appearance to the leaf. Fresh mid-green, veins light green.

'HIBERNICA VARIEGATA'

Despite the extent of its use and planting, the tetraploid form of *helix* has produced few variations; however a variegated form was in existence as early as 1859, for the catalogue of Henderson & Sons of St John's Wood, London, listed 'H. hibernica foliis elegans variegata'. Further references are found, as 'hibernica variegata', in the 1860 catalogue of Peter Lawson of Edinburgh, in the 1867 catalogues of the German firm, Haage & Schmidt, Charles Turner of Slough, England, in 1868, and Thomas Warre of Tottenham, London, in 1877, all without any adequate description. In 1872, however, Hibberd in *The Ivy* described the plant as *Hedera* grandifolia pallida, 'The pallid large-leaved ivy (syn. Golden Blotched, Hibernica, fol. var., Aurea maculata, Canariensis var. aurea, Golden-Blotched Irish ivy). This is well known, and deservedly so, for its beauty. It differs from the type only in its variegation which occurs irregularly in "splashes", some parts of the plant being superbly coloured, while others are green, and differ in no respect from the common "Irish Ivy". The variegation consists of a pale yellowish or primrose colour, with which some leaves are entirely overspread, while others are half green and half yellow, the midrib marking the division sharply; others again, are blotched and patched with variegation. This never acquires a rich variegation except when planted out, and then it is usually a noble plant, though irregularly coloured'. Hibberd's line illustration certainly depicts the plant we have today with its fairly sharp colour definitions. Not all nurseries followed Hibberd's nomenclature and the names he showed as synonyms have persisted for years.

Although Bean (1973) describes it as *H. helix* 'Hibernica Aurea' and lists a further clone as 'Hibernica Maculata' thereby following Lawrence & Schulze (1942), I think the clone we have with its rather spasmodic variegation agrees with Hibberd's description. At times, however, he confused 'Hibernica' and 'Canariensis'; because of this I believe that the earlier name, 'Hibernica Variegata', listed by Peter Lawson of Edinburgh in 1860, is the valid name which clearly links the variegated form to its parent cultivar.

What appears to have been another variety is mentioned in the catalogue of Wm. Clibran & Son, Altrincham, Cheshire, of 1894 as 'H. hibernica marginata, dull gold margin'; in 1888 J. Backhouse of York listed it as having silver-edged leaves, while in 1882 the British horticultural paper 'The Garden' mentioned 'A new and remarkably beautiful variety named Hibernica marginata'. I have not seen a marginally variegated form of 'Hibernica'; possibly it became lost or indeed it may have been another plant.

The plant in circulation today fulfils Hibberd's description. When it throws variegated shoots it can indeed be a striking plant but often the variegated shoots are rare, seen amidst a mass of ordinary green Hibernica-type leaves. Worth planting on a wall or as ground cover but *not* where consistent variegation is required.

117

Habit	Vining, vigorous.
Stems	Green, brown with age. Internodes 5–7 cm.
Petioles	Green–purple, green–yellow when supporting semi or entirely yellow leaves.
Leaves	Five lobed, 5–9 cm by 8–14 cm. Lobes triangular and bluntly acute, centre lobe larger and more prominent, sinuses shallow, base cordate. Dull matt-green, some leaves entirely yellow or parti-coloured often defined by veins, some leaves with slight broken variegation. Generally a predominance of all-green leaves.

'IVALACE'

This is an outstanding ivy unlikely to be confused with any other; this being so it is surprising that it has circulated under many erroneous names; names that are not synonyms in the true sense of the word but rather just mis-applied: they include, 'Green Gem', 'Laceveil', 'Lace Leaf', 'Wilson' and 'Little Gem'.

For a brief description it is hard to best the first, that of Bess L. Shippy (1955):

> Mr William's 'Ivalace' is a most enchanting ivy. The medium-sized bright green leaves are five lobed and the margins are finely crimped, making the edging look like fine lace. The young branches, which are produced freely stand upright until 7 or 8 inches long.

'Mr Williams' is Keith E. Williams, a wholesale florist in Springfield, Ohio, who introduced 'Ivalace' to the trade. I do not know the source, but it has something of the characteristics of 'Green Feather' and may be a mutation of that ivy. It was introduced into Europe around 1958 and has become universally popular as a pot plant. In Germany a mutation from 'Ivalace' has resulted in 'Stuttgart', another good clone.

'Ivalace' is a good all-purpose ivy; the upright branching habit noted by Mrs Shippy makes it an excellent pot plant. It is reasonably hardy and can be used as ground cover for small areas. It is excellent for low north-facing walls where it will make a curtain of glossy green, lacy leaves.

| Habit | Vining, but readily self-branching. |
| Stems | Purple-green. Internodes 1.5–2.5 cm. |

| Petioles | Purple-green. |
| Leaves | Five lobed, 4–6 cm by 4–5 cm. Centre lobe acuminate, lateral lobes sharply acute. Leaf margins strongly undulate, sinuses shallow, leaf margin convolute at the sinus cleft giving a crinkled 'lace' effect. Colour dark green, a lighter bright green on indoor plants. Leaf texture stiff, upper surface glossy, veins light green. |

'KÖNIGER'S AUSLESE'

One of the most popular varieties for house-plant use, this clone originated in Germany and was being grown under the name 'Heraut' in Belgium in 1952, but some German nurserymen claim it to have been grown in Germany as early as 1935. It has been sold, incorrectly, as 'Königer', 'Königer's Rhum' and 'Sagittifolia'. Van de Laar (1965) has drawn attention to its propensity to vary and has suggested that the original has been superseded by variations. The plant sold as 'Sagittifolia' in Britain is probably one of these. In my observations it differs only in having a tougher, slightly smaller leaf. A plant named 'Feastii' growing in the Oxford Botanic Garden has a marked affinity to 'Königer's Auslese' and it may well be that 'Königer's Auslese' is a straight development of *Hedera helix* and not a descendant, as so many house-plant type ivies are, of the self-branching 'Pittsburgh'.

Habit	Self-branching.
Stems	Green-purple. Internodes 1–2 cm.
Petioles	Green-purple.
Leaves	Five lobed, 3–7 cm by 5–8 cm. Centre lobe twice as long as laterals. Lobes tapering acuminate. Basal lobes back pointing. Colour mid-green, veins light green, not pronounced, veins of lateral lobes often make a right angle with centre vein.

'KOLIBRI'

This valuable and decorative clone arose as a mutation from 'Ingrid' (syn. 'Ester') during the 1970s on the nurseries of Firma Brokamp of Ramsdorf, Westfalen, Germany. The clone 'Ester', said to have come into commerce in 1959–62, was a variation of the better-known 'Eva' and certainly the similarity to 'Eva' is seen in 'Kolibri'. The most striking feature is the extent and whiteness of its variegation, against the white ground the flecks and spots of mid-green stand out sharply. This colour combination is supplemented by pink to light purple stems and petioles. The plant is very close jointed with rather pointed leaves. All these factors combine to make an excellent pot plant for room, greenhouse or conservatory decoration.

Habit   Self-branching and short jointed.
Stems   Pink-purple. Internodes 1–1.5 cm.
Petioles Cream-pink, seldom over 2 cm.
Leaves   Five lobed, 2–4 cm by 2–4 cm. Basal lobes not promi-
         nent. Centre lobe acuminate and one-third longer than
         the bluntly acute lateral lobes. Basic colour white-cream,
         irregularly splashed and flecked mid-green with
         occasional flecks of grey-green. Veins not prominent,
         cream or light green.

'KURIOS'

This interesting clone, the result of a mutation from 'Shamrock', was isolated by Brother Heieck at the garden of Neuburg Monastery near Heidelberg and named by him in 1979. 'Kurios' is similar in leaf type to 'Big Deal' but differs markedly by its thick fasciated petioles and its stiff branching habit which is similar to that of 'Big Deal' but less zig-zag. An ivy of individuality it makes a fascinating pot plant and a point of interest in any ivy collection.

Habit   Stiffly branching.
Stems   Thick and comparatively rigid, purple. Internodes 3–
         7 cm.
Petioles Fasciated and greatly thickened in comparison to other
         ivies, 4 mm width compared to the average of 2 mm.
         Colour green-purple.
Leaves   Unlobed, rounded to a blunt slight apex. 4 cm by 4–5 cm.
         Surface wrinkled and concave or convex on different
         leaves. Colour medium green. Veins radiating from the
         visible petiole/leaf blade-junction, becoming purple on
         older leaves.

The origin of this popular self-branching clone is not known but since it occasionally throws shoots that resemble 'Glacier' it may have been a mutation from that widely known clone. Whatever its origin 'Little Diamond' or 'Kleiner Diamant' as it is known in Europe has been grown certainly since the late 1960s. Rather too slow-growing for commercial growers it is a useful pot plant and one of the variegated ivies suitable for rock gardens where variegated ivies are accepted. The leaves, closely set on the stem are diamond-shaped, the base colour grey-green with good white variegation. As plants mature the little shoots assume an almost arborescent form the leaves tending to 'spiral' in the way they come off the stem rather than in the two rows of the young shoots. I have seen no evidence of flowering and this semi-adult state with its diamond-shaped leaves similar to the adult leaves of other ivies seems normal to this interesting clone about which little is known.

Habit	Self-branching.
Stems	Green. Internodes 0.25–1.5 cm.
Petioles	Green, short, rarely more than 3 cm.
Leaves	Unlobed, 3–4 cm by 1.5–2 cm. The acute apex and attenuate base give a diamond-shape leaf with a few leaves showing vestigial lobes. Grey-green variegated with white mainly at the edges. Primary veins raised.

'LITTLE GEM'

An attractive little ivy whose small leaves and fairly close habit make it suitable for ground cover over bulbs in small areas. If the vining stems are pinched back it makes a useful pot plant and can be used as a climber for moss-sticks. A mutation from 'Pittsburgh', 'Little Gem' was noted by van de Laar in 1952 and named and described by him in 1965.

Habit	Self-branching.
Stems	Purple, somewhat stiff. Internodes 1.5–2 cm.
Petioles	Red-purple, the colour extending a short way up the centre vein and visible both on the under and upper leaf surfaces.
Leaves	Three lobed, 3–4 cm by 4–4.5 cm. Basal lobes vestigial

or absent. Centre lobe acute, lateral lobes less so. Leaf base deep lying so that the leaf folds slightly upwards at the base, the centre lobe tends to point downwards. Colour medium green, veins light green with the red-purple coloration extending 0.5–1 cm up from the petiole junction.

'LOBATA MAJOR'

The names 'Lobata' and 'Triloba' have been applied and mis-applied over the years. It is likely that both are types that arose in the west of Britain where *helix* has produced forms with larger leaves, often part way to 'Hibernica'. The following description is based on plants at the Royal Botanic Gardens, Kew, and which broadly coincide with Hibberd's (1872) description of the plant he called 'Lobata Major'. Lawrence & Schulze (1942) were correct in saying that this is not a very distinguished clone. It is now seldom offered by nurserymen but may be found in old gardens and in the wild in Britain. 'Feastii' is probably a similar plant.

Habit	Vining.
Stems	Green-purple. Internodes 5–6 cm.
Petioles	Green-purple.
Leaves	Three lobed, 4–8 cm by 5–11 cm. Two basal lobes always present to a greater or lesser degree. The lateral lobes at right angles to the long, acuminate centre lobe. Similar in leaf structure to 'Pedata' but the leaf is larger, dark green and the lighter green veins not prominent, whereas in 'Pedata' they are a primary feature.

'LUZII'

This plant originating at the Ernst Luz nursery in Stuttgart-Fell-bach, was put on the market by the firm of Hausmann and exhibited at the Hanover show in 1951. It has given rise to a number of simi-larly mottled clones but remains a valuable variety in its own right, grown by the million for the house-plant trade. Its lightly mottled leaves are sufficient to look different and the plant is more forgiving of ill treatment such as neglect in bars and hotels than more highly variegated varieties. Essentially a most useful house-plant ivy, if planted outside it loses some of its mottle. Described by Nannenga-

Bremekamp (1970) as 'Luzii' it is variously misnamed as 'Lutzii', 'Lutzei', 'Minima Luzii' and sometimes 'Marmorata'.

Habit   Self-branching.
Stems   Purple-green. Internodes 2–3 cm.
Petioles   Purple-green.
Leaves   Five lobed, 3–4 cm by 3–4 cm. Lobes not pronounced, auriculate and tending to overlap slightly. Centre lobe rather longer than lateral lobes. Colour light grey-green mottled and speckled yellow-green.

'MANDA'S CRESTED'

In many families of cultivated plants there arise varieties that become virtually 'classics', plants of character. Pioneers, they often break new ground. Among Hederas two such are 'Green Feather' and this one, 'Manda's Crested' as it was described by Bates (1940). One of a number of mutations from 'Merion Beauty' noted on the nurseries of W. A. Manda Inc., South Orange, New Jersey, and introduced by them, 'Manda's Crested' was the first of the 'curlies', clones in which the leaf sinuses have an upward curvature while the lobes point downwards giving the attractive curly effect. The plant was introduced to Europe and in Britain given the erroneous, albeit descriptive, name of 'Curly Locks'. Names apart, it is a superb ivy for troughs, pots or baskets indoors or for ground cover outside where in winter it attains its delightful coppery winter colour. Its thin leaves indicate a certain tenderness; in Britain it has survived − 12°C (10°F) with no problems, but suffers far more from cold winds.

Habit   Self-branching but vining sufficiently to make slowly spreading cover.
Stems   Green-purple. Internodes 2–2.5 cm.
Petioles   Green-purple, comparatively long – 7–8 cm.
Leaves   Five lobed, rarely reduced to three, 5–6 cm by 7–8 cm. Typically star-shaped, basal lobes back-pointing and almost the same length as the lateral lobes, this with the overlap of the basal lobes makes the petiole junction appear to be at the leaf centre. Sinuses very shallow, all five lobes convolute with blunt down-pointing apices

giving the characteristic curly look. Light, almost pea-green, veins lighter but not prominent.

'MAPLE QUEEN'

A mutation from 'Pittsburgh' this long-established clone was introduced by Mr Sylvan Hahn of Pittsburgh, Pennsylvania, and issued with the United States Plant Patent Number 429 on 15 October 1940. An easy grower, the medium, rather variable-sized dark-green leaves are typical of most people's idea of ivy while the red-purple stems make a pleasing contrast. A reliable, trouble-free indoor ivy for pots, troughs or baskets, it is reasonably hardy surviving $-7°C$ ($19°F$) and cold winds in Britain. According to Pierot (1974) it can be grown outdoors as far north as New York City. The ivy sold as 'Kobby' is the same plant.

Habit   Self-branching with short trails.
Stems   Purple-red. Internodes 2–2.5 cm.
Petioles Purple-red.
Leaves   Three lobed, 3–5 cm by 3.5–5.5 cm. Centre lobe pro-
          longed, basal lobes vestigial, apices bluntly acute.
          Sinuses variable, slightly waved at the cleft. Leaf base
          truncate. Dark green with light green veins.

'MERION BEAUTY'

This clone was described in 1940 by Bates in the National Horticultural Magazine (vol. 14). It originated with Mr Henry Faust of Merion, Philadelphia, as a mutation from Pittsburgh and was introduced in 1937/8. It is striking by reason of the shortness of the internodes, this gives a most compact plant particularly useful for pot culture or topiary work. Synonyms are 'Hahn Miniature' and 'Procumbens' and it has been confused with 'Neilsonii'. This confusion is probably due to the existence of clones not representative of the plant described here. It has survived $-10°C$ ($14°F$) in Britain, but is obviously better suited as a house or cold greenhouse plant.

Habit   Self-branching and compact.
Stems   Green-purple. Internodes 1–1.5 cm.
Petioles Green.
Leaves   Three lobed, basal lobes vestigial, 2–3 cm by 3–4 cm.
          Centre lobe wedge-shaped, lateral lobes obtuse giving a

124

square appearance. Branches readily from every node. Colour mid-green, veins lighter but not prominent, generally very little pigment.

'MINOR MARMORATA'

The first person to publish a comprehensive list of ivy varieties was William Paul (1823–1905) the British nurseryman who in the 'Gardener's Chronicle' of 1867 listed, with brief descriptions, his collection of some forty kinds. The German botanist Dr Karl Koch published this list, with due acknowledgements, in the 'Gartnerei und Pflanzenkunde' in 1870; Koch had devoted some time to the genus and it was his father, Dr Caspar Koch, who discovered and named *Hedera colchica*. Paul's list had also been published in the German garden paper 'Hamburger Garten-und Blumenzeitung' of 1868. The names rapidly became accepted on both sides of the channel and formed the basis of catalogues for many years. Among those in Paul's list is 'Minor Marmorata', described as 'Leaves green, beautifully marbled with white, small, growth rapid, exceedingly pretty'.

Hibberd (1872) described the same plant, certainly with more detail than Paul, but changed the name to 'Discolor' giving 'Minor Marmorata' and 'Maculata' as synonyms. There seems no logical reason for this other than change for the sake of change or possibly a disregard for Paul as a mere nurseryman. Whatever the nineteenth-century intrigues that led Hibberd to ignore Paul's name the fact remains that it was properly published both in Britain and Germany and has priority. Needless to say most nurserymen carried on listing the plant as 'Minor Marmorata' or sometimes as 'Marmorata Minor', the name used, presumably in error, by Nicholson in his *Dictionary of Gardening* (1885) with, incidentally, quite a good illustration. Neither Schneider nor Rehder mention the plant but Lawrence & Schulze (1942) followed Hibberd and, disregarding Paul and Koch, call the plant 'Discolor'. Nannenga-Bremekamp (1970) describes the plant as 'Minor Marmorata' and the 8th Edition of W. J. Bean's *Trees and Shrubs Hardy in the British Isles* adheres to this correct nomenclature.

The American Ivy Society in its provisional 'Check-list' has followed Hibberd but doubtless further research will indicate the validity of the earlier name. Other names associated with this clone in addition to 'Discolor', are 'Maculata', 'Dealbata', 'Marmorata Minor', 'Marmorata Elegantissima', 'Marmorata Elegans' and 'Richmond Gem'.

As the foregoing shows the plant is long established; it is a typical vining *helix* type with the hardiness associated with this species. Leonnie Bell (1968) described the leaf as 'mottled or coarsely salted – white on deep green' and this well describes the variegation which to many people has a 'virus' appearance. It is essentially a wall ivy, better on a north wall; on south-facing walls it acquires a scruffy look; its young growth has colour and interest.

Habit   Vining – covering slowly.
Stems   Green-dull purple, young shoots pink-green.
Petioles   Dull purple.
Leaves   Three lobed, lateral lobes auriculated to give a deltoid shape, 3–5 cm by 4–5 cm. Centre lobe sometimes prolonged on older leaves. Base colour dark green young growth spotted and splashed with cream-white, often in slightly angular patterns. Variegation so distributed so as to cause little or no leaf distortion. Older leaves markedly more green.

'MODERN TIMES'

This would appear to be the *H. helix* 'Woodsii' of Pierot (1974). Her description and that of 'Modern Times' by Nannenga-Bremekamp (1970) coincide almost exactly, as do the excellent illustrations in both works. The description by Nannenga-Bremekamp pre-dates that of Mrs Pierot and accordingly the plant becomes 'Modern Times'. The clone was selected by Hage & Co. of Boskoop, Holland, in 1951 from 'Curlilocks' which they had imported, presumably from America.

Both writers emphasise the blunt apices and the flat appearance of the leaves, Mrs Pierot commenting on the 'velvety' green and the apple-green of the young leaves and the pale veins. I can add two diagnostic points: the centre veins of the two basal lobes are frequently at complete right angles to the leaf's centre vein, also the presence of a white 'dot' produced by the meeting of the veins at the petiole/leaf-blade junction. Reasonably hardy in Britain, Mrs Pierot says it can be grown outdoors as far north as New York City.

An excellent ivy for low walls and pleasant for any indoor use where a moderately vigorous green ivy is required.

Habit   Vining.
Stems   Green-purple. Internodes 4–5 cm.
Petioles   Green-purple.
Leaves   Five lobed, 5 cm by 5–7 cm wide. Sinuses shallow giving little length to the near equal basal and lateral lobes. Terminal lobe wedge-shaped, as long as broad, laterals blunt and rounded. Matt mid-green, veins light green to white. Centre veins of basal lobes make right angles to the leaf centre vein. There is often a white 'dot' at the junction of the veins at petiole/leaf-blade junction.

'MRS POLLOCK'

From the rather inadequate catalogue descriptions of this clone I suspect it to be the golden variegated form of what is described elsewhere in this book as 'Corrugata'. The name was often quoted as a synonym of 'Palmata Aurea' but strangely enough the first record of 'Mrs Pollock' is that of Charles Turner of Slough, England, who in 1885 listed *both* 'Palmata Aurea' and 'Mrs Pollock', unfortunately without descriptions. In 1888 J. Backhouse of York listed it as 'Vitifolia Aurea' giving 'Mrs Pollock' as a synonym. The name appeared in many catalogues and horticultural publications but descriptions varied; Barr & Sons (1895) described it as 'Bright yellow edged green and finely cut'. The weekly periodical, 'The Garden' of March 1897 said, 'Variegated well marked foliage somewhat digitate'. In 1901 L. R. Russell Ltd, of Richmond, Surrey, listed it as 'Gold blotched', while Jackmans of Woking, Surrey, in 1936 described it as 'Small leafed gold deeply indented'.

The only properly published comment is contained in Hibberd's report of the Ivy Trials held at the Chiswick Gardens of the Royal Horticultural Society (RHS Journal, Vol. 1890): 'Chrysophylla palmata is a brilliant golden leaved variety of the green leaved palmata. Contributed by Mr Fraser as "Palmata Nova Aurea". Also known in gardens as "Mrs Pollock" and palmata aurea.' Tobler (1912) recorded the name in his list of garden varieties and it appears in the *Kew Hand List* for 1925 but with no published account. At the present time there is in circulation a plant of gold variegation with all the characteristics of 'Corrugata'. If this is not the plant that was sold as 'Mrs Pollock' it is difficult to judge what variety that could have been or what variety the present plant, occasionally seen in old gardens and at the Royal Botanic Gardens, Kew, can be. An interesting and good wall ivy.

Habit   Vining.
Stems   Green. Internodes 3–5 cm.
Petioles Green.
Leaves   Five to seven lobed, 5–6 cm by 5–7 cm. Lobes often appear as little more than forward-pointing projections or large teeth at the apex of a leaf whose cuneate base makes it like an inverted triangle having its apex at the petiole junction. The lobes are short and acuminate with narrow sinuses. Medium green, blotched yellow. Veins light green, very thin and radiating closely from the petiole junction.

'NEBULOSA'

This is an ivy described and named by Hibberd (1872). He also indicated the place where he found it, 'Growing on the parapet of the bridge which spans the little waterfall in the village of Dwygyffylchi, North Wales'. An ivy still grows on the bridge and it, and cuttings taken from it conform to Hibberd's description: 'The stems are dark green when mature, purplish when young. The leaves are smallish, in form usually sagittate, reticulated with whitish veins on a green ground, or mottled and clouded with grey and yellowish white.'

It must be said that this is only a small variation of *Hedera helix*, seen in Britain and possibly in Europe, fairly frequently. Its main, indeed only distinct, feature is a slight thickening of the leaf which, with the recessed veins combine to give the 'cloudy' appearance described by Hibberd. Not a noteworthy plant.

Habit   Vining.
Stems   Dark green to purple. Internodes 2–4 cm.
Petioles Purple-green.
Leaves   Broadly sagittate, remotely tri-lobed. 3–5 cm by 5–6 cm. Leaf base slightly auriculate. Dark green. Vein light green in contrast. Substance of the leaf blade and con-

trasting colour of the small subsidiary veins can give the
leaf a 'cloudy' appearance.

A clone that is grown extensively for the pot-plant trade but whose
origin seems obscure. It appears to have arisen in Denmark, probably in the late 1950s. It is sometimes known as 'Neilsonii', but
for a clone distributed after 1959, the date of the implementation
of the rules of the International Code of Botanical Nomenclature,
this latinised form would be incorrect. The clone is similar to
'Merion Beauty' and to 'Hahn's Self Branching'; the latter clone,
an early mutation from 'Pittsburgh', is now reckoned to be synonymous with it and it seems likely that, along with 'Chicago', they
are all fairly similar. In the case of 'Neilson' it is inevitable that
a clone grown on a massive scale on a number of nurseries will,
with individual selection produce numerous forms. The following
is thought to be reasonably typical of the clone.

Habit	Self-branching and compact.
Stems	Green-purple. Internodes 1–2 cm.
Petioles	Green-purple.
Leaves	Three lobed, 3–4 cm by 3–4 cm. Two basal lobes vestigial. Centre lobe wedge-shaped at least twice the length of the laterals. Sinuses shallow, apices acute. Light green, veins lighter green, not pronounced.

'NIGRA'

The earliest description of this clone is that of Hibberd (1872)
where he describes it as a 'Dark form of pustulata ... veins less
distinctly marked, the colour much darker in the summer and in
winter deepening to almost black. This variety was received from Mr
Wills of Edgbaston.' It is doubtful as to what ivy Hibberd was
describing as 'Pustulata', but his mention of Mr Wills explains subsequent references, in particular that of Nicholson (1885) to 'Willseana' which he described as a 'Dark leaved form nearly allied to
H. helix "Lobata Major" from which it differs in the veins being
less distinctly marked and in the colour being much darker in the
summer and in winter deepening to almost black.' He gave 'Nigra'
as a synonym while Hibberd gave 'Willseana' as a synonym, which

suggests that it was known under this name before Hibberd's book was published. Doubtless, knowing it to be the older name, this was the reason for Nicholson's adopting 'Willseana' rather than Hibberd's invented name. Unfortunately there is no recorded publication of 'Willseana' before that of Nicholson (1885) which was of course pre-dated by Hibberd's 'Nigra' (1872) so, by the rules of priority in nomenclature, 'Nigra' it is.

The plant is still occasionally seen and was submitted to the Royal Horticultural Society's Ivy Trial in 1977. A good vining ivy, its dark-green leaves would make a good foil for pale-flowered wall shrubs or climbers.

Habit	Vining.
Stems	Purple. Internodes 3–4 cm.
Petioles	Purple.
Leaves	Three lobed, 3–7 cm by 3–5 cm. Lobe apices acute, centre lobe almost twice the length of lateral lobes. Leaf apex slightly down pointing giving the leaf a convex appearance. Leaf base slightly cordate. Very dark green, veins lighter in young leaves, not prominent in older leaves.

'NIGRA AUREA'

'Distinct colouring of black, gold and red.' This catalogue description of an ivy is sufficient to excite any plantsman's interest but, unless some quite extraordinary ivy has been lost to cultivation it is somewhat exaggerated. The plant which is at present under this name in a few gardens today and has been entered in the Royal Horticultural Society's Ivy Trial in 1977 is certainly copiously splashed with yellow; its basic colour is dark green, turning almost black in winter and, like many ivies, tinges of purple appear in cold weather, but this hardly adds up to 'Black, gold and red'.

There appears to be no published descriptions other than those in a few British catalogues from about 1908 until the outbreak of World War 2. It is possible that the variety 'Flava', described in Haage and Schmidt's catalogue of 1869 as 'With small yellow variegated leaves', may have been this plant. This is pure conjecture and in any event the name 'Flava', uncompromisingly yellow, would be as unsuitable a name to describe this plant as the somewhat contradictory 'Nigra Aurea', an interesting clone, similar in leaf to 'Nigra', but as one would expect of a variegated plant, not so vigorous. Suitable and colourful as light ground cover for border or rock garden.

Habit	Vining.
Stems	Purple. Internodes 3–3.5 cm.
Petioles	Purple-green.
Leaves	Three lobed, 2.5–3 cm by 2.5–3.5 cm. Apices acute, lateral lobes wedge-shaped, sometimes reduced to protrusions. Leaf base cordate. Basic leaf colour dark green. Young leaves commence green and acquire their dappled, clear butter-yellow mottle with age. Under surface tends to remain a light green. Veins pale but not prominent.

'OLD LACE'

The plasticity of *H. helix* as a species shows itself in the fair degree of frequency with which clones produce mutations with crimped leaf edges. Such a mutation is 'Old Lace' differing from the usual Parsley Ivy types in that the cell proliferation at the leaf edge is less, giving a more delicate lacy effect. A useful addition to the range of indoor ivies.

Habit	Self-branching.
Stems	Green-light purple. Internodes 1–2 cm.
Petioles	Green to light purple.
Leaves	Five lobed, but sinuses so shallow as to make them appear unlobed, 2–2.5 cm by 3–4 cm. Leaf margin lightly crimped all round. Mid-green, veins lighter, the centre vein strikingly straight in its line from petiole to leaf apex.

'PALMATA'

In the past every tree and shrub nursery appeared to list 'Palmata', albeit with little or no description. Nowadays few nurseries list it and there seems little agreement as to the typical plant.

The first listing I have found is that of Peter Lawson & Son, Nurserymen of Edinburgh, who catalogued it without description in 1846. William Paul (1867) described it as 'Dark green, medium size, very broad, deeply cleft, veins prominent, vigorous'. Over the years it was catalogued, usually as 'The five fingered ivy' or, as Jackmans of Woking, Surrey, put it (Catalogue, 1936), 'Small leafed with deeply indented foliage'. Hibberd (1872) illustrated it, writing of its 'Medium sized three to five-lobed leaves which tend to a palmate appearance'. Thereafter writers seemed to have over-looked this variety until Bean (1973) described it as 'Strongly five-lobed, truncate at base, veins prominent beneath'. If we combine this with Paul's and Hibberd's writings, we get a picture of this variety which is still found fairly frequently in old gardens and sometimes in the wild. A hardy climbing ivy, useful to plant as an alternative to the common ivy.

Habit   Vining.
Stems   Purple-green. Internodes 3–3.5 cm.
Petioles Green-purple.
Leaves   Three to five lobed, 4–6 cm by 3.5–6 cm. Centre and two
          lateral lobes equally proportioned, wedge-shaped and
          acute, basal lobes smaller. Sinuses narrow, sometimes
          convolute at cleft. Leaf base truncate. Dark green, veins
          light green, prominent on underside of leaf.

'PARSLEY CRESTED'

There appear to be no references to this clone until the 1950s although Lawrence (1956), when describing the plant, suggested it might then have been in cultivation for about twenty-five years. It seems possible that mutations having the same crimped leaf edge may have arisen in several places since the introduction of the ramulose ivy type. This may account for the several names in circulation, *viz.* 'Cristata' (Jenny 1964), 'Rokoko', 'Parsley', 'Pice Lep' and 'Crestata'. Graf (1963) illustrated it as 'Parsley Crested' and Nannenga-Bremekamp (1970) retained the same name.

In addition to its useful self-branching habit it throws trails that make it a suitable ivy for hanging baskets; a measure of root restriction tends to enhance the Parsley effect. Suitable for low walls and excellent for ground cover in small areas.

Habit   Self branching.
Stems   Green-purple. Internodes 1–3 cm.

132

Petioles	Green-purple.
Leaves	Unlobed or vestigially tri-lobed, 4–6 cm by 4–6 cm. Ovate with acute apex, to almost circular. Leaf base slightly auriculate. Leaf margin undulate with crimped edge caused by proliferation of the marginal cells. Occasionally this proliferation can occur as eruptions a little way from the margin. Colour a fresh bright green. Veins lighter and fairly prominent. The constricted leaf margin produces some puckering and undulation of the leaf surface. In Britain and possibly elsewhere the natural undulations in the foliage occasionally become colonised by a species of Eriophyid mite whose activities tend to increase the irregularities of the leaf margin (Darlington, *Plant Galls in Colour*, Blandford Press, 1968).

'PEDATA'

This, the Bird's Foot ivy, is undoubtedly a natural variant of *Hedera helix*. In a domesticated landscape such as that of Britain it is difficult to tell that which is wild from a garden escape but it seems practically certain that 'Pedata' along with other clones such as 'Lobata' and 'Triloba' are variations of *helix* that have occurred in Britain, particularly in the west, an area very conducive to ivy growth.

Whatever its origins the plant was first known as 'Caenwoodiana', certainly by 1863 when it was listed in the catalogue of James & John Fraser of Leebridge Nurseries, Essex. This name appears to refer to Caenwood House in Hampstead, London. This was the seat of the Earls of Mansfield and, shortly after 1841, the name of the property was changed to Kenwood House (this incidentally accounts for the reference in the *Handbuch der Laubholz-Benennung* (Beissner, Schelle und Zabel 1903) to *Hedera helix* 'Kenwoodiana'). The house is now a Museum (Kenwood House, Hampstead Lane). The name 'Caenwoodiana' survived for many years but mainly in catalogues. This was due to Shirley Hibberd who in *The Ivy* (1872) described the plant as 'Pedata'. Hibberd caused much confusion by changing well-known and well-used personal names to latinised descriptive ones. He does not mention 'Caenwoodiana' in his monograph but his description and illustration of 'Pedata' is obviously the same plant. Other authorities,

133

including Bean (1914) and Rehder (*Manual of Cultivated Trees and Shrubs*, 1927), followed Hibberd. The horticultural press nevertheless continued to refer to 'Caenwoodiana' and it has appeared in catalogues up to the present time.

The report confirmed 'Pedata' as the name of the Bird's Foot from the RHS Journal of 1889 on the trial of ivies held at the Society's Chiswick Gardens:

> *Hedera* pedata is one of the most distinct and interesting; the leaves are divided like a bird's foot, the grey veins are very distinct. Being rather spare and given to objectionable variations when it has mounted to some height on a wall, it is desirable to cut it down occasionally to keep it well furnished and in proper character. Sent as Caenwoodiana by Fraser and as Pedata by Turner, syn, digitata chrysocarpa, North Indian Golden Fruited.

It is no great surprise to learn that the report was written by Hibberd and the fact that he had sold his collection to Turner, the celebrated Slough nurseryman, would explain why Turner entered the variety as 'Pedata'! But despite its wide use, Hibberd did not even include 'Caenwoodiana' as a synonym.

The report confirmed 'Pedata' as the name of the 'Bird's Foot' ivy, a name accepted by Lawrence & Schulze (1942) and Nannenga-Bremekamp (1970). Apart from this historical bickering over the name, the plant itself is a reliable useful ivy. Its prime use is on walls or pillars where its hardiness, quick growth and attractive leaf pattern are so useful. The leaf coverage is not sufficiently close for ground cover. Synonyms have included, 'Digitata', 'Deltsifolia', 'Caenwoodiana', 'Caenwoodii', 'Combwoodiana', 'Kenwoodiana' and 'Weienstephan'.

Habit	Vining.
Stems	Green. Internodes 2–5 cm.
Petioles	Green.
Leaves.	Five lobed, 4–5 cm by 5–6 cm. Centre lobe prolonged and narrow, approx. 1 cm wide, and one and a half times as long as lateral lobes. Apices acuminate, sinuses wide, lateral lobes being almost at right angles to centre lobe. Basal lobes back-pointing. Dark green, veins grey-white

giving an impression of grey-green colour to the whole plant.

This clone is mainly useful as a house plant where its branching habit makes it more suitable than the more colourful but longer-jointed 'Goldheart'. The colours, however, are paler and much less well defined than those of 'Goldheart'. The plant shows little tendency to revert, unlike a similar introduction, 'Green Quartz', in which the central yellow splash reverted readily to green, so that it is no longer grown or available.

A mutation from 'Pittsburgh', selected by Brother Heieck of Neuburg Monastery, Heidelberg, 'Peter' was introduced by Gebr. Stauss, Möglingen-bei-Stuttgart, Germany, and awarded a Gold Medal at the Floriade, Amsterdam, 1974, and awards at Genoa and Hamburg.

Habit   Self-branching.
Stems   Green-pink to purple. Internodes 1.5–2.5 cm.
Petioles Green-pink.
Leaves   Three lobed, 4–5 cm by 3–6 cm. Centre lobe slightly pro-
          longed and acuminate. Laterals acute, sinuses shallow.
          Colour light green with pale green-yellow, irregular
          central splash. Veins lighter but not prominent.

'PIN OAK'

A useful ivy capable of making mounds of small-leaved ground cover or equally a good pot plant. The American Ivy Society 'Check-list' gives its origin as Merion, Philadelphia, from the nursery of Henry Faust Inc., and states that it was first marketed in 1941. 'Pin Oak Improved' from the same nursery, and alleged to be hardier, was introduced at the Philadelphia Flower Show of 1942. Stocks of 'Pin Oak' in circulation differ widely, possibly due to this introduction of two similar clones as well as to extensive propagation by a variety of nurseries. Graf (1963) drew attention to its rather weak manner of growth and red stems, the American 'Alestake Nursery' catalogue identifies this, more properly, as 'a graceful habit' and lists 'Ferney' as a synonym. Lawrence (1956) described it, and Nannenga-Bremekamp (1970), putting it in the Green Feather group, described it as 'three-lobed, small-leaved with deep sinuses'. 'Pin Oak Improved', if it can be identified, is said to have large leaves. 'Green Finger' is a rather similar clone. Of the several stocks in circulation the following is probably representative.

Habit   Self-branching.
Stems   Red-purple. Internodes 0.5–2 cm.
Petioles   Pink-green.
Leaves   Three lobed, 1–2.5 cm by 1–2 cm. Centre lobe twice length of lateral lobes. Apices acuminate, sinuses deep, leaf base truncate. Light, almost yellow-green in colour, veins not prominent.

'PITTSBURGH'

This short-jointed, small leaved ivy was the first of the self-branching ivies. It is said to have originated between 1915 and 1920 as a mutation from *H. helix* 'Hibernica' and was introduced by Paul S. Randolph of Verona, Pennsylvania, who marketed it in 1920. The assumption that it mutated from 'Hibernica' arose because Bates, the American horticulturist, writing in the 'National Horticultural Magazine' in 1932 showed that the bulk of ivy growing in N. America was in fact 'Hibernica'. I think it more likely to be a mutation from *Hedera helix*. Mutations do, from time to time, produce shoots that revert to their parent and those produced by 'Pittsburgh' do not resemble 'Hibernica' but are similar to the sharp-leaved type of common ivy found wild in Britain.

'Pittsburgh' is an historical variety since it was the forerunner of a whole race of ivies in both America and Europe which Bates termed the Ramosa complex, recognised by their branching or 'ramulose' habit and their generally thinner leaves compared with normal *helix* or indeed the other species. It has been grown on a vast scale for the house-plant trade and although somewhat superseded by newer, green, short-jointed clones such as 'Neilson' is still admirable for that purpose. It has circulated under many names including 'Chicago', 'Chrysanna', 'Hahn Self-branching', 'Ray's Supreme', 'Procumbens', 'Spitzberg' and 'Spitzbergii'.

Habit   Self-branching.
Stems   Green-purple. Internodes 1.5–2 cm.

Petioles	Green-purple.
Leaves	Five lobed, 3–5 cm by 5–6 cm. Apices acute, leaf base cordate, sinuses shallow. Leaf blade held at an angle parallel to the stem giving a stem taken from the plant an elegant appearance. Medium green, veins lighter.

'PIXIE'

There is something almost fern-like in this clone with its small, soft green, finely cut leaves. Often linked with the names 'Holly', 'Weber Californian' and 'Margaret', plants offered as 'Pixie' at the present time differ from descriptions of 'Holly' by Lawrence & Schulze (1942), Lawrence (1956) and Nannenger-Bremekamp (1970). They conform, however, to the descriptions in Suzanne Pierot's *Ivy Book* of 1974 and the reference of Graf (1963). They agree also with the American Ivy Society's 'Check-list' description of 'Weber Californian'. It seems, therefore that 'Pixie' is a different plant from 'Holly', possibly a mutation from it since the two names have been so often linked, but is the same clone as 'Weber Californian'. So much for parentage – what of the plant? It is best described as a miniature vining ivy since, although basically self-branching, it is capable of making long trails which, with its small leaves, make it very suitable for hanging baskets or elevated troughs.

Habit	Miniature vining.
Stems	Slender, purple-green. Internodes 2–3.5 cm.
Petioles	Slender, purple-green.
Leaves	Five lobed, but often having two additional vestigious basal lobes, 2.5–4 cm by 2–3.5 cm. Lobes acuminate, centre lobe prolonged, sinuses narrow, slightly convoluted at the cleft. Leaf margin slightly crimped. Light green, veins lighter.

VAR. POETICA

Most ivies are grown for the beauty and interest of their juvenile leaves; the merit of this one, however, lies in its orange-coloured fruits. For this reason it is usually seen as a small shrub or Tree Ivy having been propagated from adult or arborescent growths.

137

The plant has a long history for, according to Pliny, *Natural History* (AD 23–79), writing on ivies,

> One kind has a black seed and another the colour of saffron, the latter is used by poets for their wreaths and its leaves are not so dark in colour ... some people among the Greeks make two classes of this variety depending on the colour of the berries, red berried ivy and golden fruited ivy.

As with other species and varieties of ivy it has suffered name changes. Weston in his *Universal Botanist and Nurseryman* (1770) listed it as 'Poetica baccis luteis – Yellow berried archipelagian ivy'. The Rev. Robert Walsh collected the plant near Constantinople and described it as *chrysocarpa* in a paper read to the Royal Horticultural Society on 6 July 1824 and published in the Society's Transactions of 1826. Later, in 1835, Bertoloni described it as 'Poetarum'. All three names appeared in catalogues and publications as well as *lucida, baccifera lutea* and *Fructo-luteo*, bestowed by various writers. Lawrence & Schultze (1942) followed Weston in calling it var. poetica. In the 8th Edition of Bean (1973) it is now 'var. poetica' in place of the *chrysocarpa* of previous editions, the name used, surprisingly, by Nicholson (1885) to describe what we now call *H. nepalensis*, a totally different ivy from a totally different region.

Being accustomed to the black fruits of most arborescent ivies, the orange fruits of var. poetica are of immediate interest, but some people comparing them with those of pyracantha or cotoneaster will find them dull. Pliny spoke of a 'Red berried ivy' as well as a 'Golden fruited ivy'; it is possible that variations in fruit colour exist and anyone making a study of the plant in its Eastern Mediterranean habitat might be able to select forms of varying fruit colour, including perhaps the white form, leucocarpa, reputed to exist but so far as I can tell, never described.

H.h poetica is seldom seen in cultivation now but was widely grown in Hibberd's day. In his book *The Ivy* he described with some enthusiasm a pot-grown bush in his own garden saying that the 'Clusters of berries on the plant selected (and illustrated) numbered forty-two'.

Habit   Vining.
Stems   Light pink to green. Internodes 4–5 cm.

Petioles	Pink-green.
Leaves	Five lobed, 5–7 cm by 6–8 cm. The two basal lobes much reduced giving a rather 'square' leaf. Lobes broadly acute, centre only slightly longer than laterals. Leaf base cordate, leaf has a slight tendency to upward folding. Colour, light almost yellow-green. Petiole colouring often follows into the veins and is seen both above and below the leaf surface.
Fruits	As seen on small pot specimens, dull orange.

PROFESSOR FRIEDRICH TOBLER'

This very distinctive clone was selected by Hans Schmidt of Bockum-Hövel in Germany and introduced at the BUGA (Bundesgarten-schau) Horticultural Show in Cologne in 1957. It is named after Professor Friedrich Tobler (1879–1957), sometime Director of the Botanic Garden, Dresden and author of the monograph *Die Gattung Hedera* (1912) and other writings on *Hedera*. It is most fitting that this interesting and unusual ivy should be named after one who contributed so much to the study of the genus.

The plant is unusual in that most of the leaves are split into three or five 'part leaves'. In this way many leaves comprise three separate leaflets, each with its own sub-petiole united to the primary petiole. The plant is moderately vigorous and will throw long trails which make it very suitable for hanging baskets. It has circulated under various names including 'Dreizehn', 'Green Ripple', 'Pedley's Green Finger', 'Pointer', 'Tobler' and 'Weidenblattrig'.

Habit	Self-branching but throwing vining trails.
Stems	Red-brown. Internodes 1–3 cm, extending to 5 cm on trails.
Petioles	Red-brown, up to 1 cm but often so short that leaves appear to be sessile.
Leaves	Variably three to five lobed, but generally completely divided into three almost linear leaflet-like lobes, each with a minute sub-petiole. The central leaflet 2–4 cm by 0.5–1 cm wide. Subsidary leaflets 1–3 cm by 0.3–0.5 cm wide. Leaflets have a strong centre vein. In some leaves leaflets are joined near the petiole junction making a more normal but deeply cut leaf. Medium green with

139

lighter green veins sometimes tinged with red towards the petiole/leaf-blade junction.

'RALF'

Rounded lobes are the chief feature of this self-branching ivy. The clone was selected by Gebr. Stauss of Möglingen near Stuttgart, Germany, and received a Gold Medal when exhibited at the 1974 Amsterdam Floriade. The plant's compact growth and neat foliage make it a useful pot plant. It is suitable also for light ground-cover.

Habit   Self-branching.
Stems   Purple-green. Internodes 1–2 cm.
Petioles Green-purple.
Leaves   Generally three lobed with, rarely, two additional small
          basal lobes; 2.5–4 cm by 3–4 cm. Lobes rounded, sinuses
          shallow. Leaf base deeply cordate. Light green; veins not
          pronounced. In outdoor situations or under stress of
          drought or cold the primary veins take on a purple
          coloration.

'ROMANZE'

This decorative ivy is an interesting selection from 'Luzii' made by Brother Heieck of Neuburg Abbey, near Heidelberg, and named by him in 1979. The curly leaves have some resemblance to 'Manda's Crested' but have a discreet mottle within the apple-green colouring. This suffused mottle combined with the more than usually numerous *helix*-type hairs on the leaf surface give the leaf a velvety appearance. A first-rate ivy for pot-plant work; not suitable for use outside.

Habit   Self-branching.
Stems   Pink-green. Internodes 1.5–2.5 cm.
Petioles Pink-green. Tend to be long, 5–8 cm.
Leaves   Five lobed, 3–5 cm by 4–5 cm. Margin waved, con-
          voluted at the sinus cleft. Centre lobe down pointing,
          basal lobes auriculate so that petiole appears to be at the
          leaf centre. Leaves so waved and curled that lobing is
          indistinct. Light apple-green with slightly darker green
          mottle.

One of the several unusual almost bizarre ivies that have appeared in recent years, 'Rüsche' was selected in 1968 from the clone 'Professor Friedrich Tobler' by Brother Heieck at Neuburg Monastery, near Heidelberg. The name has a link with the English 'Ruche' meaning a ruffle and the French 'Ruché' or frilling. The name is well chosen and descriptive of the frilled collar effect of the leaves which tend to clasp and surround the stem at the nodes. The plant is fast growing and throws long trails making it suitable for hanging baskets. It has proved hardy in Britain but is probably seen to best effect as an indoor ivy.

Habit	Vining, fast growing.
Stems	Green to brown-purple. Extending to make long trails. Internodes 2–5 cm.
Petioles	Wine-red, maximum length 2 cm but often non-existent.
Leaves	Basically five lobed, but often tri-sectional because of the deep sinuses that sometimes divide the leaf. Lobes wedge-shaped, the acute tip often down pointing. The division of the leaf and the twist of the lobes often make it appear to clasp the stem. Colour mid-green, veins lighter with a touch of red at the petiole/leaf-blade junction.

'RUSSELLIANA'

One of the erect ivies with a long history, although seldom seen now. I was told by the late Mr John Russell, VMH that in the past they grew an erect ivy unlike the present-day 'Erecta'. A study of early Russell catalogues revealed descriptions of an erect ivy listed as 'Russelliana'. The Russell Nurseries specialised in ivies around the turn of the century, and in 1900 their list included, ' "Russelliana", somewhat similar to the preceding [this was "Minima", now known as "Congesta"] but a little larger and columnal in growth with perfectly dense, small foliage of a pleasing light green'. The same name and description appears in other Russell catalogues. Other firms in later years listed a yellow ivy as 'Russelliana' but this, I suspect, was confusion with 'Russell's Gold' a yellow-leaved clone grown by the firm. *Hedera helix* 'Russelliana' drifted out of favour and was lost by the firm during World War

2; a plant was, however, discovered in a garden in Milford, Surrey, by Mr Bill Archer who recognised it as a different form of 'Erecta' and grew it in the botanical supply unit attached to Holloway College, Egham, Surrey. For garden purposes it is similar to 'Erecta', not quite as strong growing, but with larger leaves than 'Congesta'.

Habit   Non-climbing, erect.

Stems   Short jointed, usually without adventitous roots, green. Internodes 0.5–1 cm.

Petioles   Light green.

Leaves   Unlobed, ovate to reniform, 3–4 cm by 3–6 cm, arranged in two ranks, leaf margins slightly waved in young leaves, occasionally in older leaves. Texture leathery, colour light green. Veins not prominent, slightly raised but same colour as the leaf.

'SAGITTIFOLIA'

This name illustrates the confusion surrounding ivy nomenclature. Shirley Hibberd (1872) described a plant which was fairly widely grown at the time as follows:

> Arrow leaved ivy, quite distinct and interesting. In growth free and wiry, running far and filling up slowly. Leaves usually bluntly three lobed, the centre lobe projecting forward in the form of a letter V. The colour is dull dark green with a few patches of blackish bronze which changes in autumn to a rich purple bronze. The principle veins are lighter green in colour and slightly raised above the surface.

A shortened version of this was repeated by Bean (1914).

Confusion has arisen because the same name has recently been applied, in error, to a small-leaved self-branching ivy. It seems possible that, when in the late 1940s this short-jointed, arrow-head ivy made its appearance, plantsmen turned to Bean and without too much thought, called it 'Sagittifolia'. The name would have seemed appropriate and this very useful ivy was, and still is, extensively propagated for the pot-plant trade, a use incidentally for which the true 'Sagittifolia' would be useless.

The original 'Sagittifolia' is a moderate-growing, rather open plant, useful as a darker variation of the common ivy. Suitable for walls and trees, but not as ground cover. It is not generally listed by nurserymen and the plant exists only in a few large gardens and public parks where nineteenth- and early twentieth-century plantings have remained undisturbed. Hibberd and the 1914 Edition of Bean spelt the name as Sagittaefolia. I have followed the 1973 Edition of Bean and also Dr W. T. Stearn's 'Botanical Latin' in my spelling which accords with the botanical code rules.

Habit   Vining.
Stems   Dark green-purple. Internodes 3–3.5 cm.
Petioles Green-purple.
Leaves   Sagittate in outline, 3–5 cm by 4–6 cm. Centre lobe pro-
          longed, laterals short and blunt forming the wings of the
          'Arrow' and often overlapping at the base. Basal lobes
          vestigial, veins not prominent.

'SAGITTIFOLIA VARIEGATA'

An excellent self-branching ivy having small Bird's Foot type leaves. The name shows the vagaries of plant nomenclature. It is not, as might be thought, a variegated form of the true 'Sagittifolia'. That name, given by Hibberd (1872) has in recent years been used to describe a self-branching clone more akin to 'Königer's Auslese' than to the plant of Hibberd. Accordingly, when a variegated form appeared it was understandable that it should be named and described as 'Sagittifolia Variegata'. This name and description was published by van de Laar (1965) and Nannenga-Bremekamp (1970). Comparison with 'Königer's Variegated' shows it to be the same plant, but 'Königer's Variegated' has not, so far as I am aware, been published as a name, and certainly not prior to 1965; accordingly, the name 'Sagittifolia Variegata' stands, although the plant bears no resemblance to the true unvariegated 'Sagittifolia'. However, as Shakespeare phrased, it 'A Rose by any other name would smell as sweet' and this ivy, whatever its name, is a charmer and a fine plant for troughs, hanging baskets and as a pot plant. Outside it will drop some leaves in Britain in hard weather but seems to survive frost better than many variegated clones and can be used on low walls and as gentle ground cover on rock gardens.

Habit   Self-branching and close growing.
Stems   Green-purple. Internodes 0.25–1 cm.

Petioles	Green-purple, generally short.
Leaves	Three lobed and small, 2–2.5 cm by 2–3 cm. Two basal lobes vestigial or where present, back pointing. Lobes acuminate, centre lobe prolonged to twice the length of lateral lobes. Central portion grey-green, irregular border of cream-white. Veins light green, those of the lateral lobes often make a right angle with the centre vein.

'SHAMROCK'

This, the Clover Leaf Ivy, may well have been a mutation from 'Green Feather' to which it bears some resemblance, indeed Nannenga-Bremekamp (1970) places it in the Green Feather Group. Very distinct in leaf form it was introduced from the USA into Holland in 1954 and thence to the rest of Europe, becoming a popular house plant for which purpose it is excellent. Sufficiently self-branching to be used for topiary, it throws short trails making it suitable for hanging baskets or moss-sticks. Reasonably hardy but best as an indoor plant.

Habit	Self-branching with short trails.
Stems	Green-purple. Internodes 1 cm.
Petioles	Green-purple.
Leaves	Three lobed, centre lobe broad wedge-shaped, 2.5–3.5 cm by 2–3 cm. Apices blunt, often rounded. Sinuses shallow, but in some leaves split to the centre vein giving a three-leaved effect. Lateral lobes sometimes folded in pleated fashion alongside the centre lobe. Colour dark green with trace of lighter green along veins. The purple of the petiole often extending into the lower part (0.5–1 cm) of the centre and/or lateral veins on the upper side only.

'SINCLAIR SILVERLEAF'

A short-jointed clone whose small leaves display a range of variegation. The young leaves emerge pale cream-yellow; some remain that colour, others gradually become light green while yet others assume a faint green mottle, so fine that it is like a green smudge. A compact, colourful and useful pot ivy. Not recommended for outside.

Habit	Self-branching, compact.
Stems	Purple-pink. Internodes 0.25–1 cm.
Petioles	Green.
Leaves	Three lobed, 1.5–3 cm by 2–3 cm. Centre lobe wedge-shaped. Sinuses shallow, leaf base truncate to slightly cordate. Basic colour cream-yellow, mottled light green in varying degrees, some leaves entirely green. Veins cream to light green, not pronounced.

'SMALL DEAL'

Like 'Big Deal' this clone originated in America and is similar in its 'Spinach' appearance, in fact the main difference is that where the leaves of 'Big Deal' are round and entire, those of 'Small Deal' are lobed, sometimes so deeply as to give the impression of separate leaves. It is an attractive oddity for the ivy enthusiast and interesting as a pot plant. Its somewhat stiff habit precludes its use in hanging baskets.

Habit	Self-branching vining, slow growing.
Stems	Red-purple. Internodes variable, 3–4 cm where close growing but 7–8 cm on trails. Leaves often in pairs at nodes.
Petioles	Red-purple.
Leaves	Five to seven lobed, 4–5 cm by 3–5 cm. Sinuses variable, some lobes divided almost to the petiole. Apices blunt or rounded, leaf blade stiff, surface puckered. Dark green, veins thick and prominent although not raised.

'SPECTRE'

Aptly named, for this clone with its long, almost claw-like leaves with streaked yellow variegation has an almost spectral appearance. Its origin is uncertain but its introduction to Britain is attributed to Mr Stephen Taffler a noted collector of ivies. It does not appear to have been named until listed by Mrs Hazel Key in the catalogue of Fibrex Nurseries Ltd, of Evesham, Worcester, England, as 'The Spectre' and also described by her in the Royal Horticultural Society's Wisley Handbook *Ivies* (1978). Article C.23 of the International Code of Nomenclature for Cultivated Plants proscribes the use of 'A' and 'The' so the name properly becomes 'Spectre'.

Essentially an indoor ivy, 'Spectre' would seem to be a mildly varie-gated form of 'Triton'; it is certainly of great interest to ivy enthu-siasts and a worthwhile pot plant.

Habit	Branching and sprawling without any climbing charac-teristics.
Stems	Purple-green, twisting and slightly zig-zag, non-climb-ing, hairs few and scattered. Internodes 1–2 cm.
Petioles	Wine-red, often twisted.
Leaves	Three to five lobed, 5–7 cm by 2–4 cm. Sinuses deep and narrow, some leaves divided almost to the petiole. Lobes separately curled and twisted with the acuminate tips curling downwards. Mid-green streaked with faint yel-low. Veins prominent fanning in parallel fashion from the petiole/leaf-blade junction.

'SPETCHLEY'

The botanical epithets minor and minima have been applied in the past, mostly incorrectly, to various ivies; had the terms not been so used they would certainly fit this plant whose leaves can justly claim to be the smallest. Because of this past confusion it seems better to use a purely vernacular name. The plant's origin is obscure; it was certainly growing around 1962, in the gardens of Spetchley Park near Evesham in Worcestershire, but seems to have been subsequently lost. Some material certainly originated from there, subsequently appeared in several British gardens and worked its way into a limited circulation.

An interesting and useful little plant, capable of covering small rocks with its minutely leaved shoots. With age it sometimes throws more normal leaves, but these can be removed, almost in the fashion of bonsai gardening, to preserve its miniature character. Suitable for small rock gardens as stone cover, limited ground cover or indeed as a bonsai ivy.

Habit	Dwarf vining.
Stems	Purple. Internodes 0.5–1.5 cm.
Petioles	Purple.
Leaves	Remotely three lobed, 0.5–2 cm by 0.5–1.5 cm. Leaves variable from three lobed with the centre lobe prolonged, to just a single elliptic or tri-angular lobe. Blade slightly

canaliculate. Dark grey-green; due to the small leaf size the pale-grey centre vein seems prominent and the leaf texture thicker than it is. Occasional 'Off-type' shoots have internodes 1.5–2 cm and leaves 2–3 cm by 2.5–3 cm.

'STIFT NEUBURG'

This fascinating ivy was selected by Brother Ingobert Heick at Neuburg Monastery, Heidelberg, in 1962 from the clone 'Bruder Ingobert' also raised in the Monastery nursery.

'Stift Neuburg' because of its striking leaf formation and colour is essentially a house-plant ivy although it has proved hardy outside in Britain, surviving − 9°C (16°F). The raiser describes it as an interesting variety for the enthusiast and this it certainly is with its sharply variegated white and light green, crinkled, round leaves and pink stems. It is a fine pot plant ivy but probably too slow growing for commercial use.

Habit   Vining, moderately branching, growth slow to medium.
Stems   Pink to red-purple. Stiff and initially elevated from the plant until extended growth brings them to soil level.
Petioles   Pink-purple.
Leaves   Orbiculate, 2–3 cm by 4–5 cm. Leaf margin irregularly undulated with vestigial lobes showing as indentations. Leaf blade wrinkled and undulating, leaf base cordate. Colour bright green substantially splashed with white, mostly at leaf centre. Veins white or light green slightly pink in winter.

'SULPHUREA'

This useful clone was described by Hibberd in *The Ivy* (1872) and also in his commentary in the Royal Horticultural Society's Journal of 1890 on the trial of ivies held in the Chiswick gardens of the Society. It was listed in nurserymen's catalogues of the day but presumably declined in favour for it was no longer listed after World War 1 and seemed lost until the discovery by staff from the Pershore Agricultural College of a plant at Spetchley House near Evesham, Worcestershire, a stately home with gardens largely planted at the turn of the century. The plant was distributed from Pershore initially as 'Spetchley Variegated', and later its true name was realised and described in the RHS Journal for February 1975. Since its re-introduction it has proved to be a good clone for ground cover and a good wall ivy. It is as hardy as the common *H. helix* standing up well to frost and cold winds.

Habit	Vining, filling up well and providing good wall cover.
Stems	Purple-light green. Internodes 2.5–3 cm.
Petioles	Purple-light green.
Leaves	Basically three lobed, sinuses shallow, sometimes non-existent. The variegation being mostly at the leaf margin causes a certain amount of leaf puckering and concavity. This with the lack of distinctive lobing gives often a somewhat mis-shapen leaf. An ear-like protrusion is often present, mostly at the right hand of the leaf base as observed from the petiole. This was observed by Hibberd and is diagnostic of this clone. Colour, grey-green with some darker patches, becoming greyer and more sulphury in older leaves. Yellow areas of indefinite shape almost always at the leaf margin. Leaf blade on average 4–7 cm by 6–8 cm giving in general leaves broad in appearance.

'TELECURL'

This appears to be a similar clone to 'Little Picture' which was described and figured by van de Laar (1965). It was derived from 'Curlilocks' in 1953 but distributed under the invalid name of 'Nana'. I have grown both clones and am certain they are identical. According to Pierot (1974) it is likely that 'Telecurl' was a mutation from 'Merion Beauty'. This in turn was a mutation from 'Pittsburgh'; 'Curlilocks' was imported into Holland from America and most probably a mutation from 'Pittsburgh' so it is not surprising that the same clone should have arrived in different places. 'Telecurl' was noted by Lawrence in 1956; the name therefore pre-dates that of van de Laar and becomes the correct name. The convolute and deeply folded bright-green leaves make this an excellent pot plant and it throws out sufficient trails to be suitable for hanging baskets, too. Pierot (1974) says that it can be grown outside south of New York. In Britain and northern Europe it needs a sheltered corner unless the winter is mild.

Habit	Self-branching with short trails.
Stems	Green-brown. Internodes 1.5–2.5 cm.
Petioles	Green-brown.
Leaves	Five lobed, acuminate, 2–3 cm by 3.5–4 cm. Sinuses narrow, leaf blade curling upwards at the cleft. Apex of centre lobe often down pointing. Leaf blade folded upward from mid-rib. Bright green, veins fairly pronounced with some red coloration in winter at petiole/leaf-blade junction.

'TRES COUPÉ'

This clone was introduced into Britain from France. The story goes that Mr Maurice Mason, a keen British amateur gardener, saw the plant in the garden of Roger de Vilmorin of the well-known French nursery firm. Accepting the generously offered plant he enquired the name: 'Je ne sais pas,' replied his host, 'Il est tres coupé' and 'Tres Coupé' it became. It was introduced to the trade by the late Mr John Russell of L. R. Russell Ltd, of Windlesham, Surrey, in 1968.

The name describes the clone well. It is variable in leaf size and shape and may be a selection from the clone, erroneously termed in recent years, 'Sagittifolia' which in itself closely resembles 'Königer's Auslese' or 'Heraut' as it is known in Belgium. Care in the selection of propagation material is essential to maintain the short-jointed, cut-leaved characteristics. An excellent house plant for pots, baskets or topiary it is also suitable for low walls and moderate ground cover.

Habit	Self-branching.
Stems	Purple-green. Internodes 0.5–1 cm.
Petioles	Green-purple.
Leaves	Three lobed, 1–4 cm by 1.5–3 cm. Very variable, some leaves show two reduced basal lobes, making a five-lobed leaf, others may be reduced to one or two attenuated lobes. In the average leaf sinuses are wide, centre lobe twice the length of laterals, apices acuminate, leaf base truncate. Colour mid to dark green. Veins lighter and prominent.

Many ivies, both green and variegated, take on red or purple coloration under conditions of low temperature. This phenomenon was mentioned by Paul in the 'Gardener's Chronicle' in 1867 and was investigated on a scientific basis by Tobler in 1912 (*Die Gattung Hedera*), who identified various clones that coloured more readily than most. Of the variegated ivies, only this one, so far as I know, consistently retains some pink colour; even in summer the cream-yellow and grey-green leaves have a pink edge whose colour intensifies in winter. A small-leaved ivy of rather wiry slow growth it is colourful for low walls or situations where vigorous growth is not required.

The plant was known as 'Tricolor' as long ago as 1866 when William Dillistone of Munro Nursery, Essex, and Charles Noble of Sunningdale Nursery, Surrey, were among those who listed it. From then to the end of the century and later, many nurseries in Britain and on the Continent catalogued it as 'Tricolor' although with sketchy or non-existent descriptions. Hibberd (1872) described the plant in detail, but as 'Marginata rubra', listing 'Tricolor' as a synonym. This was the first proper description of the plant but it was unfortunate that Hibberd did not adhere to the name in current use. His change led to increasing confusion. Unexpectedly, since Hibberd's name had been very widely used, Lawrence & Schulze (1942) published the name 'Tricolor' with a proper description. The Royal Horticultural Society's *Gardener's Dictionary* (1951) and Hillier's *Manual of Trees & Shrubs* (1971) followed this lead. Bean (1973) lists, surprisingly, what appears to be the same plant as 'Marginata Elegantissima' taking this name from Paul's 1867 description, 'Leaves green, broadly margined with white'. It is my opinion that the plant in circulation today has a cream-yellow border rather than white and agrees more with the catalogue descriptions, albeit sketchy, of 'Tricolor'. Other synonyms include 'Argentea Rubra', 'Cullisi', 'Marginata Cullisi', 'Latifolia Elegans' and 'Silver Queen'.

Habit	Vining, slow growing.
Stems	Green-purple to dull brown. Internodes 1–2 cm.
Petioles	Purple.

Leaves   Small, 2–4 cm by 2–3 cm. Triangular, unlobed or with only vestigial basal lobes. Colour grey-green centre with irregular cream-yellow edge. Leaf margin generally with a thin pink edge, the colour intensifying and spreading in winter. Veins pale grey-green to cream-yellow on variegated portion.

'TRILOBA'

This name was first used by Hibberd (1872) and illustrations of two types of leaf appear in his book. Subsequently it appeared in one or two nineteenth-century catalogues and was listed by one British nursery as recently as 1927, but in all cases with little description other than 'three lobed'. Lawrence & Schulze (1942) seem to describe a much smaller-leaved plant, as do Graf (1963) and Pierot (1974); indeed the illustration in the last book is certainly not the plant described by Hibberd and which is still to be found in old gardens and collections. It is correct to retain Hibberd's name for this large-leaved vigorous variety; the smaller-leaved plant illustrated by Pierot warrants a different and vernacular name.

Habit   Vining.
Stems   Purple-green. Internodes 3–4 cm.
Petioles Purple-green.
Leaves   Three lobed, 3–6 cm by 5–9 cm. Lobes usually wedge-shaped and acute but sometimes rounded. Dark green, veins light green, leaf base auriculate.

'TRINITY'

This clone has been commercially available in Britain since 1969 but its origin is not known. It can be confused with only one other, 'Sinclair Silverleaf', but may be identified by its whiter leaf and sharper, slightly more elongated centre lobe. The non-green leaves of 'Sinclair Silverleaf' are of a honey-coloured cream, those of 'Trinity' creamy-white with the primary veins tending to retain green colour; as with some other clones this is more noticeable in shade conditions. An excellent and colourful ivy for indoor use, it will only succeed outside in favourable sheltered conditions.

Habit	Self-branching.
Stems	Green-purple. Internodes 2 cm.
Petioles	Green-purple.
Leaves	Five lobed, 3–5 cm by 5–6 cm. Basal lobes cordate and tending to overlap. Centre lobe one and a half times length of laterals, apex acuminate, apices of laterals acute. Leaf colour variable, some light green others suffused cream variegation, others cream-white.

'TRITON'

A most unusual ivy that has been grown in Britain from around 1970 onwards and listed by several nurseries as 'Green Feather', an invalid name because it was used and properly published by Bates (National Horticultural Magazine of America) in 1940 to describe a totally different plant. It has also been known as 'Macbeth', but 'Triton' would seem to be the prior and therefore the proper name.

This ivy is a fine subject as a specimen plant or for use in hanging baskets. It is hardy in Britain but because of its sprawling habit does not show to advantage out of doors. The leaves are five lobed with the three centre lobes long and twisted to fine points. The leaf colour and prominent raised veins suggest it to be a mutation from 'Green Ripple' but nothing seems to be known of its origin apart from the fact that it came from America.

Habit	Branching and sprawling without any climbing characteristics.
Stems	Purple-green, twisting and slightly zig-zag, non-climbing, hairs few and scattered. Internodes 1–2 cm.
Petioles	Wine-red, often twisted.
Leaves	Five lobed, 5–8 cm by 2–4 cm. Sinuses deep and narrow, some leaves divided almost to the petiole. The five lobes are slender and acuminate with the three centre lobes often longer and twisted to their points. Colour bright deep green. Veins prominent, fanning in parallel fashion from the petiole/leaf-blade junction.

'WALTHAMENSIS'

This was one of the ivies listed by Paul in 1867 as one of his 'Collection here, which consists of more than 40 sorts'. Paul was writing from his nursery in Waltham Cross and doubtless the name he bestowed recorded the variety's origin. Waltham Cross, a little north of London, was for the next hundred years the centre of what became Britain's largest glasshouse area producing vast quantities of flowers, grapes, and latterly tomatoes until building and other pressures dispersed most of it to the better light of the south coast. It may seem strange that 'Walthamensis', a useful small-leaved ivy figured only in Paul's list and not, so far as I can find, in any nurserymen's catalogue until comparatively recently. A possible reason may be that Paul was essentially a modest man, capable, and head and shoulders above many nurserymen of his day but unlikely to 'promote' a variety he had introduced and in any event, as time went on he concentrated on various other plants.

Paul's list was reproduced by the German botanist Koch in 1870 and var. 'Walthamensis' persisted in botanical circles and remained in circulation in Europe if not in Britain. Lawrence & Schulze (1942) record the variety with a very accurate figure as does Nannenga-Bremekamp (1970). The description by Bell (1968) summarises very well the quiet charm of the plant.

> An isolated runner of 'Walthamensis' is all stem, little leaf, yet once established on the ground it makes an even blanket 4″ deep, stems invisible a lovely fabric of sooty green, white threaded, no leaf larger than a single inch.

The plant is available in America but despite its local associations I know of no nurseryman offering it in Britain. It can be found in the grounds of one or two of Britain's stately homes and probably in the wild in Wales. A very similar form has been noted in the wild near Heidelberg in Germany.

Habit	Vining.
Stems	Purple. Internodes 3–5 cm.
Petioles	Purple, thin.
Leaves	Three lobed, 2–3 cm by 3–5 cm. Sinuses shallow, sometimes non-existent giving a triangular leaf. Apices bluntly acute, leaf base truncate. Dark dull green, veins lighter.

'WILLIAMSIANA'

Visual interest in ivies as individual plants depends on leaf colour and shape. This clone has good clear white variegation combined with delicately curled three-lobed leaves earning it the soubriquet in the Alestake Nurseries Catalogue (1978) of 'The variegated Curly!' Information as to the origin of this interesting clone seems sparse; it was listed by Graf (1963) whose description can hardly be bettered: 'Shapely and vigorous variety with 3 to 5 lobed leaves, the long tips curled downwards while edges of leaves are wavy, greenish ivory border around apple-green or gray center'.

Lawrence (1956) mentions the clone and this reminds us that although not widely known it has been with us for some twenty-three years. It is an excellent pot plant having the colour of the widely grown clones 'Eva' and 'Harald' but with attractive leaf variation. Not recommended for outside culture where the curling of the leaves does not show to effect.

Habit	Self-branching with short trails.
Stems	Green-purple. Internodes 1–3 cm.
Petioles	Green-purple.
Leaves	Three lobed, 3–4.5 cm by 3–5.5 cm. Sinuses shallow, lobes ovate, leaf base strongly cordate. Leaf blade slightly puckered, margin wavy, apices acuminate often down pointing and curled. Base colour grey-green with generous leaf margin of cream-white. Veins white.

'WOENERI'

This clone can share with 'Atropurpurea' and 'Glymii' the epithet 'purple'. Actually no ivy is purple in leaf colour but many clones take on pink or purple shades in cold weather, a phenomenon noted by Paul in 1867 and investigated scientifically by Tobler (1912). These three clones, however, can be relied upon for good purple colour in most winters, in severe weather they turn to deepest purple. I can find no trace of the name's origin but the clone is described by Jenny (1964) who states, 'probably came from Holland', but, erroneously, likens it to 'Helfordiensis'. In America it is assumed to be a synonym of 'Purpurea' but this is not so, there are sharp differences between them. A useful climbing clone, the leaves generally smaller than 'Atropurpurea' and more square.

Habit	Vining.
Stems	Purple-green. Internodes 4–5 cm.
Petioles	Purple-green.
Leaves	Three lobed, 3–5 cm by 5–6 cm. Sinuses shallow or non-existent. Centre lobe broad wedge-shaped, leaf base slightly cordate, lateral lobes almost vestigial. Dark green with lighter veins. Leaf blade turns purple in winter.

'ZEBRA'

This introduction from Gebr. Stauss of Möglingen near Stuttgart in West Germany was placed on the market during 1978. A mutation from the clone 'Harald' the name aptly describes the almost striped effect of the broken cream-yellow variegation enhanced by the way in which the primary veins radiate from the petiole/leaf-blade junction. The leaf in general is less lobed than 'Harald' with a tendency to be cupped. 'Zebra' makes an interesting and attractive pot plant.

Habit	Self-branching.
Stems	Pink-purple. Internodes 1.5–2 cm.
Petioles	Green-pink.
Leaves	Remotely five lobed, but lobes often vestigial, 2–3 cm by 3–4 cm. Colour grey-green splashed with cream-yellow often longitudinally from the petiole junction but sometimes at the leaf edge. Primary veins light yellow radiating from the petiole/leaf-blade junction in almost parallel fashion.

Hedera nepalensis

This ivy has been known under various names but for no good reason for it is a very distinct plant. It was first described as *Hedera helix* by Wallich in Roxburgh's *Flora of India* (1824); de Candolle in 1830, noting differences between it and *helix*, described it as a variety, *chrysocarpa*, a name already used by Walsh (1826) to describe what we know as var. poetica. The German botanist Karl Koch (*Dendrology*, 1853) named it a distinct species, *H. nepalensis*. Hibberd (1864) called it 'H. Himalaica' but later (1872) referred to it as 'H. helix cinerea'. Neither name had justification although *himalaica* was adopted by Tobler (1912) and *cinerea* by Bean (1914), a lapse suitably amended in the current edition of that excellent work which also lists a variety, 'Sinensis', having entire leaves as opposed to the usual 'stepped' leaf. Forms similar to this have been recently collected from Nepal, one by Roy Lancaster, Curator of the Hillier Arboretum, Winchester, and another, now registered with the American Ivy Society as 'Suzanne' (No. 753), by Dr John Creech of the US National Arboretum.

Considered to be one of the older *Hedera* species, *nepalensis* is certainly more stable than the variable *helix*, nevertheless further exploration or possibly propagation in quantity might bring different varieties or clones; a variegated form has not been recorded. Essentially a wall ivy, the sculptured down-hanging leaves and the red-brown stems make an attractive feature particularly for a north wall. Less hardy in Britain than *colchica* and *helix* but survives winters better than *canariensis*; probably hardy in USA Zone 7.

The fruit is said to be orange in colour and in this connection it is interesting to note the attractive coloured plate that appeared in the French 'Revue Horticole' of 1884 with a description by M. André of the 'scarlet fruited ivy' grown in Cannes by M. Besson, a nurseryman of Nice. M. André named his plant *Hedera helix aurantiaca* but no one else seemed to get scarlet fruits from material of this or other plants and discussion on the subject continued for some years in the horticultural press of the period. The illustration is certainly of *H. nepalensis* which does not, in my experience, fruit in Britain but may do so in southern Europe and clonal variations in fruit colour could well be possible.

Habit	Vining.
Stems	Red-brown when young to green with age. Internodes 2–3 cm. Hairs, scaly 12–15 rayed.
Petioles	Light green.
Leaves	Ovate to lanceolate, 6–10 cm by 3.5–4.5 cm. Obscurely lobed, lobes little more than projections three to six in number. Acuminate, leaf base acute. The veins which run almost parallel with the centre vein, appear as pale areas on the soft green leaf blade but are raised and light green on the leaf underside.

Hedera pastuchovii

This species was described by the botanist G. N. Woronow (Acta Instituti Botanici Academiae Scientiarum USSR. Ser. I. Fasc. I. 1933) in the following terms.

> *Hedera pastuchovii* (G Woron. In Grossh. l. c. III (1932) p. 108). Stem tall climbing, leaves leathery. On the ground shoots narrowly ovate rounded and mostly with two equal rounded lobes. Leaves on climbing stems entire or lobed, oblong or triangular, margin sometimes irregularly toothed. Basal lobes separated by a shallow notch. Apex often acute not acuminate. Petiole shorter than the blade or of the same length. Leaves on flowering branches ovate rhomboid, apex often sub-acuminate. Inflorescence un-divided or a raceme. Peduncles erect or spreading. Umbels of 15 to 20 flowers. Pedicels thin, 12–14 mm long. Calyx minutely toothed, ovate triangular, apex obtusely rounded. Berry black, spherical, style persistent, 1–1.5 mm in length.
>
> Akin to *H. colchica* (Koch) with which it may be confused but distinguished by the less leathery leaves, lobed and slightly toothed. Leaves scentless, hairs rather stellate and more like scales, berry somewhat smaller. More like *H. himalaica* (Tobler) by reason of hairs, stems and leaf indentation. Found in similar areas to colchica, Western Trans-Caucasia (Colchis).

From the material I have seen I doubt if it could be confused with *colchica* but would agree its similarity to the *himalaica* of Tobler (now *H. nepalensis*). A more detailed but similar description appears in the *Flora of the USSR* (1950). Reference to the plant was made in the Royal Horticultural Society's Journal of 1934 but there is no evidence of introduction to Britain until that made by Roy Lancaster in December 1972 from the Caspian Forest area (Khair Rud Forest) in Iran (A and L No. 26). All the plants in Britain at the present time appear to be from that introduction.

As indicated in the above description it has a resemblance to *H. nepalensis* but its garden value is probably less than that species. A plant of interest to the ivy enthusiast and specialist, it seems to be one of several species described by Russian botanists that may comprise a 'bridge' as it were between *nepalensis* of the East and *colchica* and *helix* of the West. So far it appears to be hardy in Britain and its place of origin suggests hardiness in USA Zones as far as Zone 4.

Habit	Vining.
Stems	Green-brown. Scaled. Internodes 3–4.5 cm.
Petioles	Green.
Leaves	Narrowly ovate, 4–6 cm by 3–4 cm. Apex acute to acuminate. Blade slightly cupped, margin entire, base slightly cordate. Dark glossy green, texture slightly leathery.

Hedera rhombea

In 1846 the botanists Siebold and Zuccarini recorded this, the Japanese Ivy, as *Hedera rhombea*. Over the years, however, the plant was variously named *helix, japonica, colchica* and by Nakai (*Flora Sylvatica Koreana*, 1927) as *H. tobleri*. The first reliable description is that of Bean (1941):

> A Japanese ivy of rather delicate growth, but quite hardy; the leaves are triangular to ovate, often heart shaped at the base, usually slightly three-lobed; very dark green. One form known in gardens as H. japonica variegata, has a thin marginal line of white.

Lawrence & Schulze (1942), in a detailed analysis of the various names, confirmed the early name of *rhombea*. Bean (1973) repeats the earlier description, gives Japan and Korea as its habitat and points out the *colchica*-type scale hairs of 15–20 rays.

The plant is not in general cultivation and in fact the variegated form has been the more frequently described. The many nineteenth-century references to 'Rhomboidea' refer I think to what we know as 'Deltoidea' or possibly to *helix* forms with slightly rhomboid leaves.

Habit	Vining.
Stems	Purple-green. Internodes 2–2.5 cm. Scale hairs 10–18 rays.
Petioles	Purple-green.
Leaves	Generally unlobed, ovate to triangular 2–4 cm by 4–5 cm. Texture thick, apex acute, leaf blade tending to

concavity. Medium dark green, veins recessed in the leaf blade give a 'milky' veined appearance to the leaf.

The first reference to a variegated form of the Japanese Ivy appeared in 1865 in the Belgian publication *La Belgique Horticole* where it is described as, 'A distinct green leafed variety, leaves edged with a silver band'. In 1866 the nursery firm of Dillistone & Woodthorpe of Sible Hedingham, Essex, catalogued '*rhombea* variegata, the new Japanese Ivy' also listing '*japonica* argentea, neatly edged with silver'. It was included by Paul (1867) in the *colchica* section of the varieties he grew: 'Leaves dark green, slightly but regularly margined with silver, broad and smooth. Very distinct and elegant.' In the same section he listed also, '*Hedera japonica*, leaves green, clearly and regularly margined with white, small. Very pretty, producing dense masses of foliage.'

The plant appeared in many catalogues thereafter and, in 1889, under the name 'submarginata' received a First Class Certificate in the Royal Horticultural Society's trial of ivies at Chiswick. Hibberd (1872) had named and described a variety 'submarginata' and listed '*rhombea* variegata' as one of its synonyms. From his description I doubt if Hibberd had the present plant before him. He refers to a plant with, 'Leaves ... irregular spoon shaped, with unequal lobes, the colour deep bluish green margined with a thin line of whitish variegation ... one of the best for any purpose.' The present plant is not bluish-green, is unlobed, and is not, I would say, 'the best for any purpose', but it does agree with Paul's description and with the descriptions of Lawrence & Schulze (1942) and Bean (1973). I suspect that Hibberd's 'submarginata' was the spoon-shape leaved, bluish-green, variegated ivy still to be found in Britain (there is an elderly plant at Kew) and his synonym was in error.

The early references to '*japonica* argentea' and '*japonica* variegata' in the same lists as *rhombea* 'Variegata' are a little mystifying. There is in cultivation today a variety with *colchica*-type scales and a silver edge but with thin, flat, surface veined leaves, possibly the '*japonica*' of the nineteenth century. This and the recent find of a very thin-stemmed, small-leaved green Japanese Ivy suggest that investigation into the ivies of the Far East would be most rewarding.

Habit   Vining.
Stems   Purple-green. Internodes 2–2.5 cm. Scale hairs 10–18
          rays.
Petioles Purple-green.
Leaves   Generally unlobed, ovate to triangular. 2–3 cm by 2.5–
          3.5 cm. Texture thick, apex acute, leaf blade tending to
          concavity. Medium dark green with a narrow, regular
          rim of white at the leaf edge. Veins recessed in the leaf
          blade.

Glossary of Botanical and Horticultural Terms

Acuminate   Tapering to a fine point.

Acute   Sharply pointed.

Adventitious   Normally refers to roots other than those produced from a seedling. In the ivy context refers to the roots or rootlets produced on climbing stems.

Apex (pl. apices)   Leaf or lobe tip.

Auriculate   Ear-shaped extensions at the base of the leaf.

Basal lobes   The two lower leaf lobes adjacent to the petiole.

Canaliculate   Having a longitudinal groove or channel.

Ciliate-type hairs   In ivies usually three to five hairs that radiate irregularly away from the leaf while joined at a common base.

Cleft   The bottom or innermost part of the sinus (q.v.).

Clone   Any number of plants arising originally by vegetative propagation from one plant or portion of a plant.

Convolute   Rolled with two edges towards each other.

Cordate   Heart-shaped, when the base of the leaf curves back from each side of the petiole.

Cultivar (abb cv)   An assemblage of cultivated plants which is clearly distinguishable, and when propagated retains its distinctive characteristics. A clone is one form of a cultivar.

Cuneate   Wedge-shaped at leaf base tapering to the petiole.

Cuspidate   Abruptly sharp-pointed.

Deltoid   Irregularly triangular.

Distichous   Arranged in two opposite rows.

Entire   A description usually applied to the leaf edge meaning plain or untoothed.

Genus (pl. Genera)   A convenient group comprising related species. *Hedera* is the genus to which all ivies belong.

Indumentation   The arrangement of hairs or down on a plant.

Internodes   The spaces between the nodes or joints of the stem.

Lanceolate Shaped like a spear blade.

Lateral lobes In describing ivies, refers to the lobes immediately below the centre lobe.

Leaf blade The flat part of the leaf.

Leaf base Where the leaf blade joins the petiole.

Linear Long and narrow with almost parallel sides.

Lobes Divisions of a leaf which do not go as far as the mid-rib.

Mid-rib The central vein running from the petiole to the leaf tip or furthermost leaf part.

Moss-sticks Stout bamboo sticks or plastic tubes 3.75 cm (1½ in) dia. to which sphagnum moss is tightly bound with string to make a moss-covered stick. If kept moist, house plants, including ivy, will root into and cling to it.

Mutant The product of a mutation.

Mutation Changes in plant habit, leaf shape or colour, and sometimes flower colour, can be caused by breakdowns or divergences in the cellular system. Such changes are often called 'sports' and in nature rarely benefit the plant and would normally die out. The horticulturist seeing a stem showing a new or desirable trait will propagate it and thereby raise a clone of a new type.

Node The point of union between petiole and stem.

Obtuse A blunt leaf tip.

Orbiculate Almost circular in outline.

Ovate Egg-shaped in outline.

Petiole The leaf stalk that extends from stem to leaf blade.

Ramosa *See* Self-branching.

Ramulose *See* Self-branching.

Ray hairs Minute hairs borne on growing points and young leaves and which can assist in identification.

Reniform Kidney-shaped.

Rhomboidal Similar to two triangles joined base to base.

Sagittate Like an arrow head with two equal basal lobes directed downwards.

Scale hairs *See* Stellate hairs.

Self-branching Shoots arising from every node. Ivies with this characteristic are sometimes termed ramulose or as belonging to the Ramosa group.

Sessile Not stalked; without a petiole.

Sinus The gap or division between any two lobes. A narrow sinus indicates a deep cleft with the lobes near to one another, a shallow sinus means a broad gap with lobes widely separated.

Species   Plants within a genus that have natural common characteristics which define them from other species within that genus.

Stellate hairs   Star-like hairs of from seven to twenty rays usually adpressed to the surface like scales.

Synonym   (Natural history) A superseded name.

Trails   Lengthened stems.

Truncate   Cut across, almost straight.

Varietas   Sometimes written as var. A variation or form of a species found in the wild. Both the botanical *varietas* and the term *cultivar* are commonly referred to as variety.

Vestigial   Little more than a trace of what is normally present.

Vining   Describing a plant whose shoots elongate to form long 'vines' usually with few shoots.

US Zones of Plant Hardiness

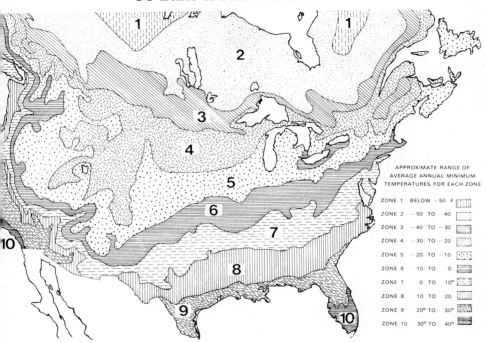

APPROXIMATE RANGE OF
AVERAGE ANNUAL MINIMUM
TEMPERATURES FOR EACH ZONE

ZONE 1	BELOW −50 F
ZONE 2	−50 TO −40
ZONE 3	−40 TO −30
ZONE 4	−30 TO −20
ZONE 5	−20 TO −10
ZONE 6	−10 TO 0
ZONE 7	0 TO 10°
ZONE 8	10 TO 20
ZONE 9	20° TO 30°
ZONE 10	30° TO 40°

Leaf Shapes

Linear

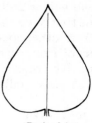

Deltoid

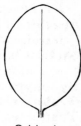

Orbicular

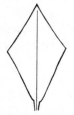

Rhomboidal

Lanceolate

Ovate

Leaf Bases

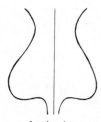

Cuneate

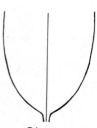

Obtuse

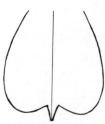

Cordate

Auriculate

Sagittate

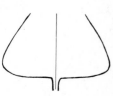

Truncate

Leaf Apices

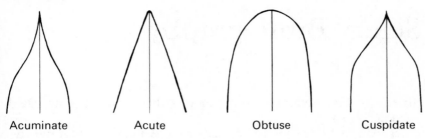

Acuminate   Acute   Obtuse   Cuspidate

The Leaf

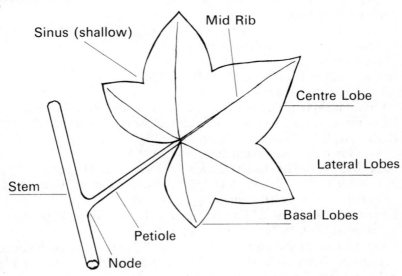

Sinus (shallow)

Mid Rib

Centre Lobe

Lateral Lobes

Stem

Basal Lobes

Petiole

Node

Select Bibliography

American Ivy Society, 'Preliminary Check-list of Cultivated Hedera', 1975.

Bates, Alfred, 'The Elusive Ivy', Series of Articles in the American National Horticultural Magazine, 1932 to 1945.

Bean, W. J., *Trees and Shrubs Hardy in the British Isles*. 1st Edition, 1914 and 8th (Revised) Edition, 1973.

Bell, Leonnie, 'The Beauty of Hardy Ivy', Morris Arboretum Bulletin, Sept. 1968.

Carriére, E. A., 'Une Importante Collection de Lierres', Revue Horticole, 1890.

Graf, A. B., *Exotica – Pictorial Cyclopedia of Exotic Plants*, 1963.

Heieck, Ingobert, *Das Efeusortiment der Gebr Stauss* – 1977 (Privately printed).

Hibberd, Shirley, Floral World, vii, 1864.

—— *The Ivy*, 1872.

Jenny, Mathias, *Jahrbuch Botanischer Garten*, Zürich, 1964.

Key, Hazel, *Ivies*. Royal Horticultural Society Handbook, 1978.

Koch, K., 'Dendrologie', Erlangen, 1869.

—— 'Gartnerei und Pflanzenkunde', 1870.

Krussman, G., *Handbuch der Laubgehölze*, Bd. II. 1977.

van de Laar, H., 'Het Hedera helix Sortiment in de Bloemisterij', Vakblad voor de Bloemisterij, May 1965.

Lawrence, G. H. M., 'The Cultivated Ivies', Morris Arboretum Bulletin, Vol. 7, No. 2, May 1956.

Lawrence, G. H. M. and Schulze, A. E., 'The Cultivated Hederas', Gentes Herbarum, VI Fasc. iii, The Bailey Hortorium of New York State College of Agriculture, 1942.

Nannenga-Bremekamp, N. E., 'Notes on Hedera Species, Varieties and Cultivars grown in the Netherlands'. Misc. Paper No. 6 of the Landbouwhogeschool, Wageningen, Netherlands, 1970.

Nicholson, G., *The Illustrated Dictionary of Gardening*, 1885 and Supplement 1901.

Paul, William, 'The Ivy', The Gardener's Chronicle & Agricultural Gazette, 1867.

Petzold and Kirchner, 'Arboretum Muscaviense', Gotha, 1864.

Pierot, Suzanne Warner, *The Ivy Book*, Macmillan, 1974.

Rehder, Alfred, *Manual of Cultivated Trees and Shrubs*, 1927.

Seeman, Berthold, 'Revision of the Natural Order Hederaceae', Journal of Botany, 1864.

Shippy, Bess L., 'The Flower Grower', Vol. 42, Sept. 1955.

Sowerby, *English Botany*, 1804.

Sprenger, 'Gartenwelt', vii, 1903.

Tobler, F., *Die Gattung Hedera*, Jena, 1912.

—— 'Die Gartenformen der Gattung Hedera', Mitt. der Deutschen Dendrologischen Ges., 1927.

Weston, R., *Universal Botanist and Nurseryman*, 1770.

Green-leaved Ivies

Hedera canariensis
,, ,, 'AZORICA'
,, ,, 'RAVENSHOLST'

Hedera colchica
,, ,, 'DENDROIDES'
,, ,, VAR. DENTATA

Hedera helix
,, ,, 'ALT HEIDELBERG'
,, ,, 'ANGULARIS'
,, ,, 'ATROPURPUREA'
,, ,, 'BIG DEAL'
,, ,, 'BOSKOOP'
,, ,, 'BROKAMP'
,, ,, 'CALIFORNIA FAN'
,, ,, 'CASCADE'
,, ,, 'CHICAGO'
,, ,, 'COCKLE SHELL'
,, ,, 'CONGESTA'
,, ,, 'CONGLOMERATA'
,, ,, 'CORRUGATA'
,, ,, 'CUSPIDATA MAJOR'
,, ,, 'CUSPIDATA MINOR'
,, ,, 'DELTOIDEA'
,, ,, 'DIGITATA'
,, ,, 'DIREKTOR BADKE'
,, ,, 'ERECTA'
,, ,, 'FAN'
,, ,, 'FLUFFY RUFFLES'
,, ,, 'GARLAND'
,, ,, 'GAVOTTE'
,, ,, 'GLYMII'
,, ,, 'GRACILIS'
,, ,, 'GREEN FEATHER'

,,	,,	'GREEN FINGER'
,,	,,	'GREEN RIPPLE'
,,	,,	'HAMILTON'
,,	,,	'HELFORD RIVER'
,,	,,	'HERON'
,,	,,	'HIBERNICA'
,,	,,	'IVALACE'
,,	,,	'KÖNIGER'S AUSELESE'
,,	,,	'KURIOS'
,,	,,	'LITTLE GEM'
,,	,,	'LOBATA MAJOR'
,,	,,	'MANDA'S CRESTED'
,,	,,	'MAPLE QUEEN'
,,	,,	'MERION BEAUTY'
,,	,,	'MODERN TIMES'
,,	,,	'NEBULOSA'
,,	,,	'NEILSON'
,,	,,	'NIGRA'
,,	,,	'OLD LACE'
,,	,,	'PALMATA'
,,	,,	'PARSLEY CRESTED'
,,	,,	'PEDATA'
,,	,	'PIN OAK'
,,	,,	'PITTSBURGH'
,,	,,	'PIXIE'
,,	,,	VAR. POETICA
,,	,,	'PROFESSOR FRIEDRICH TOBLER'
,,	,,	'RÜSCHE'
,,	,,	'RUSSELLIANA'
,,	,,	'SAGITTIFOLIA'
,,	,,	'SHAMROCK'
,,	,,	'SMALL DEAL'
,,	,,	'SPETCHLEY'
,,	,,	'TELECURL'
,,	,,	'TRES COUPÉ'
,,	,,	'TRILOBA'
,,	,,	'TRITON'
,,	,,	'WALTHAMENSIS'
,,	,,	'WOENERI'

Hedera nepalensis
Hedera pàstuchovii
Hedera rhombea

Variegated Ivies

Hedera canariensis		'GLOIRE DE MARENGO'
„	„	'MARGINO MACULATA'
„	„	'STRIATA'
Hedera colchica		'DENTATA VARIEGATA'
„	„	'SULPHUR HEART'
Hedera helix		'ADAM'
„	„	'ANGULARIS AUREA'
„	„	'ANNA MARIE'
„	„	'ARDINGLY'
„	„	'BRUDER INGOBERT'
„	„	'BUTTERCUP'
„	„	'CAENWOODIANA AUREA'
„	„	'CALIFORNIA GOLD'
„	„	'CAVENDISHII'
„	„	'CHESTER'
„	„	'CHRYSOPHYLLA'
„	„	'DEALBATA'
„	„	'DOMINO'
„	„	'EUGEN HAHN'
„	„	'EVA'
„	„	'FANTASIA'
„	„	'FLAVESCENS'
„	„	'GLACIER'
„	„	'GOLDCHILD'
„	„	'GOLDCRAFT'
„	„	'GOLDHEART'
„	„	'GOLDSTEARN'
„	„	'HARALD'
„	„	'HAZEL'
„	„	'HEISE'
„	„	'HIBERNICA VARIEGATA'
„	„	'KOLIBRI'
„	„	'LITTLE DIAMOND'
„	„	'LUZII'

Hedera helix		'MINOR MARMORATA'
,,	,,	'MRS POLLOCK'
,,	,,	'NIGRA AUREA'
,,	,,	'PETER'
,,	,,	'ROMANZE'
,,	,,	'SAGITTIFOLIA VARIEGATA'
,,	,,	'SINCLAIR SILVERLEAF'
,,	,,	'SPECTRE'.
,,	,,	'STIFT NEUBURG'
,,	,,	'SULPHUREA'
,,	,,	'TRICOLOR'
,,	,,	'TRINITY'
,,	,,	'WILLIAMSIANA'
,,	,,	'ZEBRA'
Hedera rhombea		'VARIEGATA'

Index of Ivy Names

Names and page numbers in **bold** show the varieties described in detail in this book. Species are shown in **bold italics**.

General Index